Follow The

'Wives, submit to your own husbands as to the Lord. For the husband is head of the wife, as also Christ is head of the church; and he is the Saviour of the body. Therefore, just as the church is the subject to Christ, so let the wives be to their own husbands in everything. Husbands, love your wives, just as Christ also loved the church and gave himself for it, that he might sanctify and cleanse it with the washing of water by the word, that he might present it to himself a glorious church, not having spot or wrinkle or any such thing, but that it should be holy and without blemish. So husbands ought to love their own wives as their own bodies; he who loves his wife loves himself. For no one every hated his own flesh, but nourishes and cherishes it, just as the Lord does the church. For we are members of his body, of his flesh and of his bones. 'For this reason a man shall leave his father and mother and be joined to his wife and the two shall become one flesh.' This is a great mystery, but I speak concerning Christ and the church. Nevertheless let each one of you in particular so love his own wife as himself, and let the wife see that she respects her husband.

Children obey your parents in the Lord, for this is right. "Honour your father and mother, which is the first commandment with a promise: That it may be well with you and you may live long on the earth." And you, fathers, do not provoke your children to wrath, but bring them up in the training and admonition of the Lord.'

EPHESIANS 5:22-6:4

For the best results . . .

Follow the Maker's Instructions

How to have the best in marriage and family life.

Don and Heather Double
with Peter Gammons.

Marshalls

This book is
DEDICATED
to every marriage and family
who have experienced any
difficulties, but have a desire to
find an answer.

Unless otherwise indicated, biblical quotations from the Revised Authorised Version.

Marshalls Paperbacks
Marshall Morgan and Scott
3 Beggarwood Lane, Basingstoke, Hants, RG23 7LP, UK

First published by Marshall Pickering Communications Ltd.

British Library CIP data

Double, Don
Follow the Maker's Instructions.
1. Family–Religious life
I. Title II. Double, Heather
261.8′3585 BV4526.2

ISBN 0-551-01180-7

Typeset by Ann Buchan (Typesetters)
Printed in Great Britain by
Anchor Brendon Ltd, Tiptree, Essex.

CONTENTS

Acknowledgements

I especially want to thank Peter Gammons who has diligently prepared this book. Also to Wendy, Andrea and other Team members who have worked so hard typing and re-typing the manuscript. Grateful thanks are extended to Mike Darwood, Derek Minto and Pat Darwood for reading the text and making helpful suggestions. Finally, I cannot find words to express how thankful I am to Heather, my wife, who has co-authored this book with me.

Introduction

Have you ever bought some tool or implement and started trying to use it according to your own know-how, only to find that it would not work properly? A friend of mine did that with a new computerized typewriter. The machine was supposed to erase mistakes, but when she hit the erase key it did nothing but backspace. A closer look at the instruction book revealed that the typewriter was programmed somewhat differently than had been supposed. My friend followed the book and all went well. There is a right way and a wrong way to do everything. Many commercial products carry the caution, 'For the best results, follow the maker's instructions.' This is also true for the way we should seek to live our lives. If we desire the best results, we need to obey our Maker's instructions.

When God created this wonderful universe, He considered it incomplete without a family and said, 'Let us make man in our image, according to our likeness; let them have dominion . . .' (Gen 1:26) The first family should have lived in perfect harmony and happiness. In a sinless, beautiful earth – they really had it made! But what happened? They disobeyed their Maker and everything, including their own relationship deteriorated rapidly.

Today we see that same thing happening all around us. God's instructions are either unknown or ignored, and the result is chaos!

The family is the smallest unit in a nation, but it is the most powerful. Satan knows this and is attacking the family relentlessly. One evidence of this is the dramatic increase in divorce statistics.

Many now look upon marriage as a convenience, a contract which can easily be broken if things do not go according to plan. Often, very little time or effort is put into trying to make the marriage work. Consequently, divorce becomes more readily obtainable and the rate continues to climb.

Nevertheless, the picture is not all bad. There are people today who are concerned about their families and are willing to take another look at what the Maker advises. When men and women will do that, there is no limit to what God can do for them. Today, as couples are letting Jesus be Lord in their lives, He is renewing formerly hopeless marriages and making them into something beautiful and satisfying.

1. What A Mess!

'That's it; we are through!'

Steve left, but his heart was heavy. They had both so wanted the relationship to work this time, but somehow they could not seem to make it, or at least not for more than a few months at a time, It had been like that on and off for years. Prior to marrying they had lived together, but it had been a very stormy relationship. They had hoped that marriage would bring some stability, but it had not. Things were the same as they had always been. After all, the marriage had not been built on a secure foundation. As Jane put it, 'We knew nothing about commitment.' Their commitment was only for better, not for worse! So, Steve moved to London where he found a flat, and Jane moved in with another man.

Following a series of financial disasters, Steve remembered conversations with a Christian he worked alongside whilst living in Cornwall, comments that now made a lot of sense. A growing awareness of his need of God was emphasized one Sunday as he overheard a man preaching about his relationship with Jesus at an open air meeting in London. Steve immediately began to respond to God and soon was in his car racing down to Par in Cornwall, where he planned to attend the evening service, which had already begun. At the end of the meeting, he came forward and after talking with me, took another big step in coming to the Lord. Afterwards, I encouraged him to find Jane, who was pleased to see him. Jane was still living with the other man, though she was suffering from depression much of the time, taking drugs and drinking heavily. As she put it, 'I suppose I was looking for something, but I did not know what.'

Over a meal together Steve told Jane about Sunday evening and his new found relationship with Jesus and invited her to a meeting at Par Gospel Church that Tuesday. She was neither impressed nor enthusiastic but agreed to go. It was not until they were singing the closing hymn that Jane began to hear God's voice. Someone in the congregation brought a message in tongues and through the interpretation, God spoke to her. She broke down in tears and coming forward, asked Christ into her life, 'I knew that I had been wrong all this time and that Jesus was what I had been seeking for.'

On Wednesday morning they met together in my office and were reconciled with each other and agreed to attend the 'Married Couples Weekend' which was to take place a few days later.

When Jane contacted the man she had been living with, he was shocked at her becoming a Christian and thought that she was mad, but as they had not been getting on too well, was happy for her and Steve to get back together. Amazingly, both Jane and Steve were able to get their old jobs back that same week and some friends who were out of town loaned them their home.

The weekend was a miracle of God's timing, although difficult for them in parts. They repented and asked each other's forgiveness for any hurt they had caused, going through everything they had done in the past. As Steve put it, 'Something happened to us over that weekend, God was beginning to knit us together and mould us from two people into one. Before, "For better or for worse, till death us do part", were just empty words, a formality we went through so that we could legally live together. This time we meant it!' Later, they re-took their marriage vows, at a service at Par, which was more moving than most marriages I have taken part in and sealed it with the giving of new wedding rings.

Several years have passed since then. Steve and Jane now have a good marriage, their own home and two lovely children. They recently testified at church concerning God's ability to turn what seemed like a hopeless situation to good, saying, 'Get yourself right with God, and build your marriage His way, then you won't go wrong.'

2. Firm Foundations

The sign 'Wedding Rings for hire', recently seen in a jeweller's shop window, though I am sure written in jest, sadly reflects the serious situation in our land. Divorce figures have escalated, and for may now, marriage is regarded merely as a convenience that can easily be broken. Christians, are not immune to Satan's all-out attack on the family, However, God has not left us to flounder in the dark. He really is concerned for our families. Marriage was not man's invention, but rather of the Great Architect of the universe, the one who hung the stars in space. A universe so vast that most of it is impenetrable. A cosmos so perfectly set in space, that were the earth to move a fraction nearer the sun we would all burn up or were it to move a fraction away we would all freeze. Everything that God does is perfect! When He speaks on the subject of family life, He knows what He is talking about!

Modern psychologists have written books giving 'new' advice, and offering greater 'freedom' in relationships, yet a look at the results of their teaching shows that their new ways do not really work. However, God's Word, 'The Maker's Instructions', carries a guarantee of success. To disobey them results in chaos. A major cause of family problems is when members are not playing their God-ordained roles.

So much tension and physical sickness is the result of problems in the family. One doctor said to Heather and I, after we had taught on the subject of the family, 'If all the patients on my books could hear what you have taught today, and were to put it into practice, it would cut down my daily surgery by 50%.'

The Blueprint

Families have to be built. They do not fall out of the sky! People sometimes say that marriages are made in heaven. It is true that the blueprints are. But because you have a blueprint, it does not follow that you will get the finished article. If a building is to be erected, the architect envisages the design, he puts it down on paper and then hands it over to the builder, who then passes it on to the various sub-contractors and the building begins according to the plans. If the contractor refuses to abide by what was set out on the paper, he would never get the structure the architect designed. Family life has to be fashioned according to the specification laid down by the Lord in the Bible. It has to be worked at and built and that takes time. As you read the following pages, I believe that God will speak to your heart and show areas in your family relationships that need adjustment. No matter how bad these relationships may be, there is potential if you are willing to let the Lord have His way. All things are possible, including success in your family life. We serve a miracle–working God! No matter how good your marriage may be, there is always room for improvement. There is only one way to improve, we must bring our lives more into line with the Word of God and obey 'the Maker's Instructions'.

Laying the foundations

The strength of any building depends on the depth and firmness of its foundations. Family life is no exception. In one parable, Jesus told of a house that did not fall when the rain descended, the floods came and the winds blew, because it was 'founded on the rock' (Mathew 7:24-26).

However, He went on to say, 'Everyone who *hears* these saying of mine and does not do them, will be like a foolish man who built his house on the sand. And the rain descended, the floods came, and the winds blew and beat on that house; and it fell. And great was its fall.' Hearing the Lord's Word is not enough, we must hear and *obey*. Being a Christian is no guarantee for a successful marriage. If we do not put God's principles into action we are as vulnerable as those in the world.

The first foundation for a successful marriage is to surrender and totally give our lives over to the Lord. It is really only when this foundation has been laid, that the other foundations we will consider can work. A person who has truly given their life completely over to Christ will be easy to build with.

The finest illustration I know for building a husband and wife relationship is that of a triangle with the husband on one side, the wife on the other, and God at the top. A successful marriage starts with the husband and wife each seeking to get as close to God as possible. They start quite a way apart from each other, but as they get closer to the Lord, moving up the triangle, they came into a closer and more intimate relationship with each other. All emphasis and direction is God-ward rather than man-ward and yet the result is a unity of heart and mind that comes from the Spirit of God Himself.

In the Old Testament, we read of Enoch who 'Walked with God and begat sons and daughters.' (Genesis 5:22) Here is a family man, one of the most outstanding characters in the Bible, a man who walked with God for three hundred years! You may think that if Enoch had your family, he could never have kept such a testimony. Yet we read that there was a Mrs Enoch and lots of little Enochs, yet he still walked with the Lord. I have a wife and five children so I am not just talking theory. I know what havoc can be caused in a family if one member gets out of step. But one person out of step is no reason for the others to follow too.

It is no excuse for you to lose your communion with the Lord. Jesus said, 'Your joy no man takes from you . . .' (John 16:22) If your joy has gone and you have lost the sense of God's closeness, the offender is not your spouse or your child. You cannot blame anyone but yourself. True, others may be involved, but ultimately, it is you who are responsible for your own walk. The person to check up on first is yourself. You get back into step with the Lord, and the rest of the family will follow in due course. Each member, husband, wife and children need to have a personal relationship with the Lord. A really successful family life flows from each member's communion with God. In fact everything worth having in the Christian life comes from this relationship. What sort of communion does your family have with God? What sort of relationship do you personally have with Him?

Families are an important part of the Church. In fact, if you were to ask me for a list of priorities, I would say that responsibilities to the family were on a par with Bible study, devotions and other such things. When people think that they ought to be out somewhere praying, while neglecting their families, I believe they are wrong. Some think that if the Church is right, the family will be right, but this is putting the cart before the horse. It is interesting to note that in the New Testament the main instruction to husbands, wives, children and parents, is set right in the middle of the epistle that has the most to do with Church – the Epistle to the Ephesians.

There is one Church which I have visited from time to time over a period of years. Recently the members have started to enter into a new depth of relationship with each other. They have begun to get away from formality and are discovering what Church is really about. As I sat during the service before I preached, I felt there was something different from that which I had experienced there over the previous ten years. They had become a *family*! They were relaxed and enjoying one another, as well as the Lord. It was beautiful. That can never happen in the Church until it has happened in the families that comprise it.

What goes on in the family affects the Church therefore. If there is tension in the family, you will take the tension to the Church meetings with you. If there is friction in the home, you will take your friction to Church. If husbands are not right and in God's order in the family, the Church will be short of leaders. If wives are not submitted to their husband, the Church will have rebellion in it. If children do not obey their parents, the Church will be undisciplined.

I believe that one of the reasons there is so little power and effectiveness in much of Church life, is that we pretend to be one thing when we meet together for an hour or two each week, and are another when we are at home. As family life is breaking up all around us there is no greater witness for the Lord than families who are wholeheartedly living for the Lord and for each other. God wants us to be models of what family life should be, in a world that is crying out for answers.

Down to earth

The next foundation, is the need to give ourselves totally and unreservedly to our partner. Marriage is a yoking together. Commit yourselves to working out anything that God may speak to you about. The Bible teaches that a threefold cord is not easily broken, that is the love of God and the love of a husband and wife entwined together as one. With God in the centre we are going to make it. God has not left us to flounder concerning family life. His instructions are so clear and the various roles that He has ordained for us in that structure. We need to be down to earth and realistic if we are going to have good marriages and family life.

Finally, let me share three vitally important steps to getting the most out of this book:-

1. Come desiring the Lord to have His way in your life and open for Him to speak to you and change you any way

He may wish. Without this attitude, reading this book would be a waste of time. God is always right. Rebellion causes chaos in relationships. The Bible puts it on a par with witchcraft (1 Samuel 15:23). Rebellion is not something to be suppressed, it needs God's radical surgery. Man is totally incapable of dealing with rebellion, only God can. If there is rebellion in your heart towards the Lord or His word, get before Him and seek for Him to change you. Charles Finney defined repentance as 'Giving up all controversy with God and admitting He is totally right on each and every point and that the sinner is totally wrong'.

2. Come expecting to hear God speak to you and don't 'pitchfork' it to your partner, saying 'That is just what they needed to hear'. It is not our job to change our partner or family. Usually the best thing that we can do for them is to pray for them. We need to concentrate in making sure that we are playing our role correctly in the family.

3. Be open and share concerning the things that God is saying to you. I suggest that you study this book togther as a husband and wife or even as a family, so that you can discuss it, pray and work out together the things that God says. Why not, before reading any further, put it aside and pray that the Lord will meet with you in a special way as you read it.

3. Husbands And Headship

'The husband is the head of the wife, as also Christ is the head of the Church; and He is the Saviour of the body. Therefore, just as the church is subject to Christ, so let the wives be to their own husbands in everything. Husbands, love your wives just as Christ also loved the church and gave Himself for it.' (Ephesians 5:22 - 25)

Every husband should be the leader in his own household. By household, I mean his wife, children and any others who are living under his roof. The Bible says that a husband is the head of his wife. He does not have to attain to this position, or ask his wife's permission, nor does he have to 'become' the head, God has already put him there. God has anointed him to fulfil that role. You may say, 'My wife has a stronger personality and is far more gifted; she is more of a leader than I am.' This is not true! God has placed every husband in the position of headship, and created him with the ability to lead his family. He is the one who takes final responsibility for what his family becomes and the one who should provide security to the home.

Every husband needs to take his place as the head of his wife. Some men say to me, 'But my wife will not submit.' Very often, the reason why they will not submit is because the husband will not take up his proper responsibilities as the head and lead. This is a tragedy and dishonouring to God.

The Bible says that God did not make the man for the woman, but the woman for the man. Therefore, there is a

God-given desire in a woman to be covered and to be led by her husband. The Bible makes it clear, 'the head of every man is Christ, the head of woman is man, and the head of Christ is God.' (1 Corinthians 11:3) This is God's chain of command. The man's authority extends to everything within the family. 'As the church is subject to Christ, so let the wives be to their own husbands in *everything*.' (Ephesians 5:24)

Many husbands opt out of this role with disastrous effects on their families, manifestations of which are insecurity, tension, migraines, headaches, various psychiatric problems and even nervous breakdowns. As husbands, we will one day account to the Lord for what our family becomes.

This does not mean that the husband is superior to his wife. Neither does it mean that he is better, but that God, who made them both has designed them for specific roles, Only as both partners move in their God given roles, can they find fulfilment. You will find that a woman who is trying to 'wear the trousers' will have all sorts of problems. The reason for this, is that she is trying to fulfil a role that God did not equip her for.

Family Devotions

The husband, as head, is responsible for the spiritual welfare of his family. There is much truth in the statement, 'The family that prays together, stays together.' I am so glad that when Heather and I went on our honeymoon, the first thing that we did when we arrived at the place where we were staying, was to kneel by our bed and pray together. I thank God we layed that foundation, and we still seek to pray together every day.

Do not leave it to your wife to be in the position of 'priest', in the home, even if you think she is more spiritual than you. If your wife really is more spiritual than you, then you need to seek God about it and determine by His grace to rectify the matter. When you show a willingness to take the lead, the chances are, your wife will breathe a sigh of relief and gladly step down.

Each day as a family, after the evening meal, we meet together to pray and read a portion from God's Word. *Each* member of the family prays right down to the youngest. It is beautiful to see the simple faith and expectancy of children's prayers. In our home, spending time with the Lord together is so natural.

We began by praying around the table, one at a time, starting with a different one each time. That got us going, but now it has become quite spontaneous and often a person will pray more than once. Sometimes the gifts of the Spirit flow, or we have a time of worship. After we have read a passage from Scripture, we will each share what the Lord has said to us through it or discuss what God spoke to us about individually, during the Sunday morning service. Husbands, it is your responsibility to arrange family devotions. They should be exciting, a time that the family looks forward to and not a chore. Variety is important, especially with young children. There are a number of very good family devotional books available.

Every crisis we have ever had, has been met at these family times. A situation that seems to be insurmountable to parents, when taken in the light of the Scripture, 'bear one another's burdens,' (Galatians 6:2) and shared with the family, is often seen in its true perspective. We can then unite in faith together and see God move in that situation. For 'If two of you agree on earth, concerning anything that they ask, it will be done for them by my Father in heaven' (Mathew 18:19).

One day while I was away on tour, Heather ran out of money. Joel asked her for some bananas before he left for school. She explained to him that she had no money and so he would have to pray and ask the Lord to provide some money so that she could buy the fruit. During the day, Heather was given some money and so she made the purchase. When Joel came home she gave him a banana, explaining that the Lord had answered his prayer, to which he replied, 'How did He do it? Did he throw the pennies out of the sky?'

When Stephen was sixteen and approaching the time to leave school, he felt strongly that he should get a job in banking. So we all agreed in prayer about this and he wrote off to the local banks. However, he received the same reply from them all, 'Not yet. We are not employing any sixteen year olds this year.' Each suggested that he should attend college and take a B.E.C. course and then re-apply in two years time. However, we refused to accept defeat as we strongly believed that God was indicating otherwise. So we continued to pray. He then went for an interview with a bank to which he had not previously applied and was immediately offered a job. Back at school when his Careers Officer asked him what he wanted to do on leaving school, he informed them that he had already got a job in a local bank. They told him that he must be mistaken, and at the most could only have an interview. They refused to believe that he had actually got a job locally, as so many had applied for jobs in the bank and had been informed that none were available. Added to this, we live in the second highest area of unemployment in the country. They were so convinced that he only had an interview that they wrote this on his report!

Each family needs to find their own identity and flow as God leads them in their devotional times. They do not need to be long times but every part of the family should be involved, including extended family and any who come to stay in your home. Do not leave it to the Sunday school teacher to train your children, it is your job. It is on your knee that they should learn of the Gospel.

Recently I was staying in a home where the whole family had been converted, except for the husband. He was a very influential man and director of a top company in this country. That night he heard me preach on this subject and unexpectedly brought it up after supper. As we were discussing how important it is to pray together he suddenly and quite unexpectedly, got up, gripped my hand with real emotion, took the hand of another member of the family and said, 'Let's start now.' It was a beginning, and on the last night of the crusade, he was wonderfully saved.

Husbands, give leadership to your family in everything, especially in spiritual matters. Set them an example in your longing to get to know the Lord more. Maybe you need to start having family devotions. It will take discipline to get down to starting, but there is no better or easier time to start than today.

Where Now?

Headship also means giving direction to the family. So many marriages drift into routine and become dead, dry and formal. Our marriages should be exciting, and can be if the husband's place is right and he brings direction. When was the last time that you led your family into something new, something that you had never done before? I challenge you, get alone with God and he will give you direction. He has so much variety!

Under Christ's Lordship

Only as Christ was subject to the Father was He able to fulfil His Father's will. Likewise, only as a man is himself subject to Christ can he fulfil Christ's will as far as his family is concerned. The centurion who came to Jesus did not only say, 'I am a man with authority,' but 'I also am a man *under* authority, having soldiers under me. And I say to this one "go" and he goes and to another, "come", and he comes, and to my servant, "Do this", and he does it' (Mathew 8:9). The centurion's authority came from being under Caesar's authority. Our authority as husbands comes out of being under the Lord's. When a husband is under Christ's lordship there is an automatic flow of divine authority.

Headship not lordship

The husband's authority does not come by lording it over his wife. God does not want a man to be a dictator in the home. I would not ask Heather to do something that is not good for her, and she knows that, so it is easy for her to submit. Neither does submission mean that she cannot share with me, if she feels that I am wrong. Very recently I was going to do something, which I was both determined to do and convinced that God wanted me to do. I did not even tell Heather, but she discovered it in a letter that came for us while I was away. She wrote just a little note on the back of the envelope when she sent it to me which said, 'Are you sure this is right? Do you remember when we got married, God gave us a prophecy and He said this, this and this?' That was the voice of God to me! I heard God in my wife and it was then my turn to submit. I was not submitting to Heather, but I was submitting to God. She had become the voice of God to me.

Your wife has been given to you by God as a helpmeet. If you resist that help you will miss so much of what God has for you.

This does not mean that you are easily manipulated or emotionally blackmailed into making decisions against your better judgement. We need to be beyond manipulation. However, let us ensure that we do not get hard-hearted in this. Even if your loved one sins by seeking to manipulate you, that is no justifiable ground for hurting them. There is an important place for talking things through and hearing your wife's mind in the making of decisions. We are to lead our families not drive them. God wants the husband to be a leader, who leads by love and by example.

This was recently emphasized to me when I became aware of a problem in Stephen's life. I was getting ready to deal with it, but as I talked to the Lord first, He said to me, 'It's your problem not his.' Surprised, I replied 'What do you mean, Lord. He is doing it.' The Lord said, 'Yes, but look at yourself.' I did and had to repent. I never said a word to Stephen but within two or three days he changed. If you want to know what you are like, look at your children. You are a leader and they will follow you, even in the bad points. Be a man of your word. If you say you'll do something, do it. To not do so is lying and sin. How do you expect your children to believe you when you tell them God's Word is true and that He keeps His promises, if you break yours? The practical outworking of this truth may well involve disciplining yourself to do a number of jobs you've been putting off.

Heart Submission

If you start saying to your wife, 'You have got to submit to me,' it will not work, in fact it is a recipe for disaster. Your part is to obey the Bible's instruction to husbands, and to take up your responsibilities. Her part is to obey God's instructions to wives. Husbands, God has called you to be leaders in your homes. Too many husbands are following their wives or children. The Church is bereft of leaders, because husbands are not leading in their homes.

The Bible makes it clear that the husband cannot properly play his role in the Church if his family is not in order. For 'If a man does not know how to rule his own house, how will he take care of the Church of God' (1 Timothy 3:5). In fact, if your relationship with your wife isn't right, your whole prayer life and relationship with God will be adversely affected.'Husbands, dwell with them with understanding, giving honour to the wife, as to the weaker vessel, and as being heirs together of the grace of life, that your prayers may not be hindered' (1 Peter 3:7). God gives you the authority to be the head in your household. You do not have to work at it or attain to it. You have it! Ask my family and those who live in my home who has the authority. They know. But ask them how much authority I wield, and the answer will be 'hardly any'. I do not need to throw my weight around.

Authority is like soap, the more you use it, the less you have.

If you have not been taking the lead before, repent and ask your wife to forgive you and by God's grace seek to start to day. Give your family the security of knowing that they have a head.

4. Little Things Mean A Lot!

'Husbands, love your wives, just as Christ also loved the Church and gave Himself for it' (Ephesians 5:25)
'So husbands ought to love their own wives as their own bodies: He who loves his wife loves himself. For no-one ever hated his own flesh, but nourishes and cherishes it, just as the Lord does the church.' (Ephesians 5:28-29)

As husbands we are called to love our wives in the same way as Christ loved the Church, when He gave Himself for it. That is a high calling, and very different from the picture presented to us by Hollywood and the things which we see on our television screens. Let us not compare ourselves with how others behave. God has given each of us a model of how to love our wives, that model is Jesus. It may seem a high example to follow but we will never get anywhere unless we have that goal.

To love like this is to be willing to lay down your life for your wife and to realize that she is the most important person in your life. I meet so many wives who are starved of love.

Even if you feel you have a difficult wife, it is good to remember that God loved us when we were unlovely. Your wife may not be the 'perfect woman' you thought she was when you married her, but you should still love her as Christ loves the Church. Even today Christ loves the Church with all of its imperfections. Love has a transforming effect and makes submission easy. So the more you love your wife, the easier it is for her to submit to that love and the more harmonious and happy your life together will be.

Love is not just gushy emotions, but practical. So what are the outworkings of a love like this? When I was a young man, the song that was 'Top of the Pops' was called 'Little things mean a lot!' How true that statement is in our family relationships. So as we look together at the following list, let us honestly consider how we measure up to it, open and eager for God to change us.

1. Tell your wife every day that you love her. I travel a lot in ministry and spend over 50% of my time each year apart from my wife. Yet even when I am hundreds of miles away I telephone her every evening to tell her that I love her. If I am in the African bush, where it is impossible to 'phone her, I write her a letter every day and include telling her that I love her. Wives need to hear this from us. Don't just take it for granted or assume she knows!

If you want the right welcome when you come home at night, make sure you give the right farewell before you leave in the morning. Leave your wife looking forward to your homecoming.

2. Show by your actions that you love your wife. Little things do mean a lot. It is not enough to show affection on special days such as wedding anniversaries and birthdays. In marriage counselling, I find that when things have gone wrong, it is usually not the big things, but the little things that have been neglected. No woman can hold out long against a man who takes note of the little things. By little things I mean, for example, buying your wife flowers from time to time. Flowers are important to any woman.

In one crusade, we saw quite a remarkable effect from this teaching on the family. The next day the local florist was inundated with business. Eventually the shop manager asked one of his customers, 'What is going on. Why are all these husbands coming in here buying their wives flowers?' The man procedded to tell him that the evangelist at the tent crusade had preached on this the previous evening. To which the florist replied, 'If his preaching has this effect, I had better go along myself and see.' And he did!

If your wife is not dieting, buy her a box of chocolates. To unexpectedly buy her favourite perfume is another way of showing her how much you care. Every so often take her out for a special dinner or a week-end away, alone. Make it your business to find out the things that please her and make sure she gets plenty of them. Be creative. The ideas are endless. Keep the element of surprise alive in your marriage. It is these 'little things' that help to keep a freshness in your relationship. Perhaps it could be just a little kiss on the cheek while she is doing the washing up.

Remembering her birthday and your wedding anniversary is very important. I know one of one couple who have a celebration meal together each month on the aniversary day on which they were married. Sometimes they go to a restaurant, but other times they have a special meal at home by candle-light. As the children have grown up they have come to accept this as a normal occurrence and gladly let their parents have one evening a month to themselves. It is not always possible to buy an expensive meal out or even to make a lavish one at home, but a simple meal, lovingly prepared, in a romantic setting, can be one of these little things that mean a lot.

If your wife asks you for a dress, take her out and buy her two! For the Scriptures say 'If someone asks you for your cloak, give him your coat also. Go the second mile'. The answer of course is to keep your wife well supplied so that she doesn't have to ask. If you feel that you cannot afford that kind of treatment, ask the Lord to provide a miracle for you. He is our true source and His resources are limitless. He can afford it! These things are too important to let slip by. When was the last time you took your wife out and bought her some item of clothing, without her either having to ask for it, or because it was Christmas or her birthday?

The principle that I am really getting at is *thoughtfulness*. It is the little things that count.

3. Let your wife know that you delight in her. She needs your encouragement and to know constantly that you find pleasure in her. Don't just praise her when you are alone together, but do so in front of others, especially your children. Let them know that they have the best mother in the world. Never be verbally destructive to your wife. Rather, watch what God is doing in her life and encourage her by telling her when you see something good happen.

Heather and I enjoy each other's company. There is no area of my life that I do not want her to be involved in. She is my best friend and I am hers. We have two holidays a year, one by ourselves and one with the whole family. I look forward to both and would not want to miss either. Basically, because we enjoy being together.

4. Help build her faith. Encourage your wife to use her faith to get answers to her prayers and to believe God to supply for her personal needs. Do not misunderstand me, it is our responsibility to provide for our wives. The Scriptures clearly teach that a man who does not provide for his own family is worse than an infidel. However, there may be some things which she desires, that are not necessities, things she could do without, but which she would like in the home. These are the things that it might be good for her to reach out in faith for, rather than relying on you to supply them.

I have found that the children soon catch on with this too. When my son Stephen was only about five years old, he wanted some red wellington boots. (Don't ask me why!) We said, 'You pray and ask Jesus for them', which he did. The next day someone knowing nothing about this, took him out and bought him a pair of red wellington boots. Imagine the impression that made on his young life.

You are responsible to teach your wife and family how to use their faith and to be an example to them in this area. The principle being, that if God chose to take the husband home first, the wife should be able to stand in her own faith in God.

5. *Protect her*. 'Likewise you husbands, dwell with them with understanding giving honour to the wife, as to the *weaker vessel*, and as being heirs together of the grace of life; that your prayers may not be hindered.' (1 Peter 3:7). After travelling around the world, I am convinced that this does not primarily refer to the wife being the weaker vessel physically. In some areas of the world, the wife does all the work. She tills the ground, milks the cows, looks after the animals, runs the home and bears as many children as it is possible to produce. In fact, she is very likely to work to the moment of confinement and then almost immediately resume her work.

After watching the kind of work women in Africa do, I am convinced that by 'weaker vessel' the scriptures do not primarily mean weaker physically. 'Weaker vessel' means the weaker one emotionally. It is the husband's responsibility to protect his wife by taking pressures off her. One of the things this involves is taking financial responsibility from her. I do not believe that any woman should have the financial worries of the home. Even if the wife is the book-keeper, it is still the husband's responsibility as head to see that the finances are there to pay the bills.

When your wife's period comes around, that is the time when she needs extra care and understanding, especially from a couple of days before. I keep an account in my diary so that I can make special allowances and provide that extra care for my wife at this time of the month. If I find her getting a little uptight, I know why. It is not because we have fallen out, but that she just needs that extra care and understanding. So many husbands are insensitive in this area, which causes a build-up of tension, until their wife explodes, then they blame her, responding 'Oh no, not again'. By sensitively caring for your wife, you can do a lot to relieve these situations.

6. *Be observant*. It is very important to be observant and to let your wife know that you have noticed things. When she cooks you a very nice meal, imagine the hurt caused by

just coming home, scoffing it, and then leaving her to do all the washing up, without even saying 'thank you.' We should watch out for those occasions when our wives go out of their way to please us, have worked really hard in the home or done something special with the children and make sure that we thank them. These courtesies are often given to friends and visitors, but forgotten in the home.

For example, my wife had a new hairstyle some time ago. When she came home, I couldn't honestly say that it turned me on, but I did say, 'It is different' (and it was). At least, I did not have to tell a lie and pretend that I liked it, but I did let her know that I had noticed. When your wife re-arranges the home while cleaning it, be observant, notice and encourage her.

7. *Be a good listener*. Your wife needs to know that she has access to your time and that you are willing to listen to her and will go out of your way to understand her. It is amazing how many people have been married for twenty or thirty years and yet still do not understand their wives. Many involved in ministry will freely give time to counsel and listen to the problems of others yet won't listen to the problems of their own wives.

I was interested in an article I recently read which gave a new slant to the text, 'The wife does not have authority over her own body but the husband does. And likewise the husband does not have authority over his own body, but the wife does.' (1 Cor. 7:4). The Scripture was taken out of its context, but a valid point was made. An ear is part of the body and we should let our wives have power on our ears and listen to what they have to say.

Spend time together; many marriage problems are caused because people's Church activities are given a higher priority in their lives than their marriage and family life.

Giving time to the family is not the same as giving time to your wife. You may say, 'We are part of a church with lots of activity.' I believe you should give your prime time to your wife. Find time to be alone with her and do things together. I was counselling a couple recently who had been married for quite a number of years, yet as we were talking the Lord said to me, 'The problem is that the wife is still looking for a husband.' When I said this, she burst into tears. They were two people living under the same roof, sleeping in the same bed, but living independent lives. One of the first goals that I set them was to cross some of the things in their diary out and put in time to spend with each other.

A major cause of marriage problems today is the increasing demand for employees to travel or live away from home for long periods of time, for example lorry drivers or those who work on oil rigs.

If a marriage is not built strongly before this happens, it will never get built under those conditions. Also, the temptation to have an affair will be high. It is better to seek alternative employment even if this means lowering one's standard of living to have a happy marriage, than to have a job that causes strain and pressure on the relationship. For 'Better is a dry morsel with quietness, than a house full of feasting with strife' (Proverbs 17:1). 'Better is a little with the fear of the Lord, than great treasure with trouble. Better is a dinner of herbs where love is, than a fatted calf with hatred.' (Prov. 15:16 & 17)

Only after the relationship has been built strongly, might it be right to resume travelling, if this is the call on a person's life.

8. Be considerate. We need to be good-mannered towards our wives. Open doors and help her with her coat. Make sure she is seated comfortably at the table before sitting down yourself. Do not forget to introduce her to others. Make sure that you immediately introduce your wife, and let her feel that she is really wanted whenever she is around. So many wives feel unwanted, except for convenience, as a servant in the home or to look after the children.

Make sure that you dress and smell in a way that is attractive to your wife. It is so important to me to know how Heather likes me to dress and what deodorants she likes me to wear. I want to please her.

Another practical point is to keep your bedroom tidy. Avoid those things that irritate your wife. The way to do this is to be open with each other and make it your business to find out those things which annoy her. Ask her to be open and then make sure that you do not do those things again. You will find that it will have a remarkable effect in your marriage.

9. *Make sure that your wife is sexually fulfilled.* 'The wife does not have authority over her own body, but the husband does. And likewise the husband does not have authority over his own body, but the wife does. Do not deprive one another, except with consent for a time, that you may give yourself to fasting and prayer; and come together again so that Satan does not tempt you because of your lack of self-control'. (1 Cor. 7:4-5).

In counselling couples, I have found that so many marriage problems and all sorts of symptoms stem from problems in their sexual relationships. Irritability, bad temperedness (especially with the wife and children) and an inferiority complex are often symptoms of a poor sexual relationship. For many people, over-activity in business, hobbies and even church activities are an effort to find fulfilment and satisfaction, the root of the trouble being in their sexual experience.

Too many men, when it comes to sexual relationships, are selfish. Our number one motive should be to fulfil our wife and to bring her to a climax, not merely to bring ourselves to orgasm. I believe that sexual relationships came under the curse at the Fall, the same as every other part of life. However, it is God's will that every couple should have complete fulfilment in every way, no matter how much you have failed in the past or for how long. I have known those who have failed in this area for a great number of years, who, with the Lord's help, have got it right and now enjoy a full sexual experience, so it is something you can get down and pray about in faith. God is interested in your sex life and wants it to be of the highest quality. After all it was His idea in the first place, not yours! '*The Act of Marriage*', by Tim and Beverley LaHaye, is a superb book on this subject, which has been tremendously helpful in bringing couples who have problems in this area through to success.

The best fulfilment in sexual relationships is the result of loving each other from first thing in the morning until last thing at night. The husband should not expect his wife to just 'switch on' when they go to bed at night. Love making is not just something that happens when you get to bed. It should be the climax of the whole day spent for each other, showing love in the little things. Your welcome home to each other, conversation over meal times and actions throughout the evening are so important. During the day one partner at least is usually accessible by phone. Make the most of the time you do have together.

We need to realize the difference between a husband and wife emotionally. Whilst a man can be turned on by seeing his wife undress and immediately be ready for intercourse, a woman is aroused sexually through touch. We need to discover the things which stimulate our wives. As God has made each woman different, so each woman differs in the way she is aroused.

Husbands, has your love grown cold? Can you remember a time when you loved your wife more than you do now? Then you need to seek God to renew that love in you once again. If a man does not love his wife, he cannot love God. If a man cannot treat his wife properly, he will lack reality in his Church life. His worship will certainly be substandard and if he has any sort of ministry it will lack power and effectiveness. Much spiritual activity can be nothing but hypocrisy. When we get our homes right the Church will become effective in reaching our world, which is in such a mess as far as family life is concerned. If we get our own families right, others will be queuing up at our doors to find out where the secret lies.

I believe that these nine practical outworkings of love

will help to transform any marriage in which the couple has a basic desire to attain God's best.

Ten Commandments for Husbands

1. Thou shalt love thy wife, as Christ loved the Church, laying down thy life for her so that she may become mature in Christ. (Eph. 5:25.)
2. Thou shalt be considerate to thy wife, for God did not intend her to bear undue emotional pressure. (1 Peter 3:7.)
3. Thou shalt forgive thy wife, *never* bearing grudges. Forgive her as God forgave thee. (Eph. 4:32 & Col. 3:13.)
4. Thous shalt lead thy wife and family into the paths of righteousness, imparting spiritual life and godly fear to them. (Eph. 5:23.)
5. Thou shalt be the head of thy family, giving them proper security, love, fatherhood and protection, as God intended. (1 Cor. 11:3.)
6. Thou shalt live joyfully with thy wife, remembering that she is God's gift to thee. (Genesis 2.)
7. Thou shalt bless and praise thy wife, telling her that she is the best wife in the world. (Prov. 31:28 & 29.)
8. Thou shalt trust confidently and believe in thy wife in order for her to be the wife God wants thee to have. (Prov. 31:11.)
9. Thou shalt lovingly communicate to thy wife all the desires of thy heart, practically showing thy appreciation of her. (Eph. 4:29.)
10. Thou shalt keep thyself for thy wife, devoting thyself only unto her. (Rom. 12:10 Eph. 5:31 and Mal. 2:15.)

5. An Exhortation To Wives

(Don)

'Likewise you wives, be submissive to your own husbands, that even is some do not obey the word, they, without a word, may be won by the conduct of their wives, when they observe your chaste conduct accompanied by fear' (1 Peter 3:1-2.)

As we have already considered, being a Christian is no guarantee for a successful marriage. If we do not put God's principles into action, we are as vulnerable as the world. Someone once said that many wives work so hard to make good husbands that they never quite manage to be good wives.

God's first word to wives is 'Therefore just as the Church is subject to Christ, so let the wives be to their own husbands in *everything*.' (Eph. 5:24). Yet so many wives say, 'I will submit to my husband in most things' or 'I will submit if I feel led to'. However, neither of these statements are scriptural. Many wives wish that word 'everything' was not in the Scriptures. But it is. It is there in the original Greek and in every version of the Bible I have found. The only exception is if the husband requires his wife to indulge in sin that breaks God's higher law.

If a woman can honestly say, 'I submit to my husband in every single thing,' that is the sign of holiness. It is not how many tracts she can give out, how many 'words of knowledge' she received or how many meetings she attends. The hallmark of a wife's holiness is her submission to her husband.

Obedience or Submission?

We read in 1 Peter 3:6 that 'Sarah obeyed Abraham, calling him "Lord"'! If a woman submits to her husband that is a sign of her holiness! Of course, it is possible to obey without submitting. The Bible does not say, 'wives, obey your husbands'; it says, 'submit' to them. Submission is a condition of heart.

The story is told of a little child whose father said, 'Sit down'. However, the child rebelliously remained standing. The father said again, 'Sit down' but the child still disobeyed. The angered father said, 'If you don't sit down immediately, I will come and smack you.' and began to walk towards his son. The boy sat down but looked up and said, 'I might be sitting down on the outside, but inside I am still standing up.' He obeyed but he did not submit.

I believe that the saddest thing in a marriage is to see the wife leading the husband. It is dishonouring to God. It might bring the wife a selfish satisfaction, but it will not produce true godly harmony. God has ordained that the husband should be the head of the home. The Lord does not say that the husband is *better* than the wife. Personally, I would consider my wife very much better than me. But she must fulfil her clearly defined role as the Scriptures set out and I must fulfil mine; then we will have harmony. If we confuse or intertwine these roles, we will have problems. Someone has said, 'many wives like the plaque, "Christ is the head of the home", because they would rather have an invisible head than a visible one!' The husband is the head of the home and Christ should be the Lord of his life.

In homes where the husband is not taking his God-ordained position of leadership, displaying this plaque is really an insult to the Lord.

You may say, 'We are living in a different generation; we have had special laws passed in parliament.' True, but they are not duplicated in heaven. God intends the wife to submit. He created her that way. Many women are looking for liberty and fulfilment. But true happiness and liberty can only be found by obeying God and the 'Maker's Instructions'.

I knew a lady who was sixty and had been married for many years. Her husband was like a little lamb and she led him everywhere. She had everything planned out and whenever a question was addressed to her husband the wife answered it. (That is a sign of rebellion, and shows what is in a person's heart. If you are a wife like that, I suggest you pray that God will watch over your lips and change your heart so that you do not sin with your tongue again. If your husband asks you to answer the question that is a different thing). Well, the Lord eventually got through to this lady and her heart was really melted. One day, around the meal table at a conference, she broke into tears. Looking across the table at me, with tears streaming down her face, she said, 'Don, after all these years, I can see how wrong our family has been and what mistakes I have made.' I replied, 'We are about to discover the real person God made you to be.' We have! She is a changed woman! It is only as we come in line with God's word that we discover who we really are.

The Voice of God

You will never discover the person God meant you to be as a wife, until you come to the place of submission. Submission does not mean being dictated to, crushed or booted around like a football. I have already shared how Heather has often been the voice of God to me. Wives, you will often be the voice of God to your husband, but, the attitude in which you deliver the message is most important. If you are seeking to take authority in the situation or to demonstrate your superiority, then you will find yourself in trouble. Your husband very likely will not hear what God is saying. If your spirit is right, he will listen to you. Obviously, a wife may discuss issues with her husband and should do so, but ultimately, when it comes to decision making, the authority is with him, He should have the last word. *In fact, submission is not really tested until you disagree.*

True Beauty

> *'Do not let your beauty be that outward adorning of arranging the hair of wearing gold, or of putting on fine apparel; but let it be the hidden person of the heart, with the incorruptible ornament of a gentle and quiet spirit, which is very precious in the sight of God'*. (1 Peter 3:3 & 4)

Many young ladies, who were so careful make themselves attractive to win their husbands, after a while, especially after the children arrived, let themselves go. This is not godly.

In these verses Peter talks about the adorning of a wife. The ministry of 'adorning' is a wonderful one. Notice that Peter is not saying to the wife that she should not adorn herself by putting on gold, or good apparel or that she must not have a hairdo. For those who would teach from this passage that a wife should not wear jewellery or have attractive hairstyles, the obvious conclusion is that she should not wear clothes either! No, what he is saying is, 'Do not let it be only that; because if that is all you have got, it is not enough!' The wife's attitudes are far more important than her appearance.

However, I believe that it is good for a wife to dress herself up in smart, but not drab or dull clothes and to wear modest jewellery. It is good to have her hair styled attractively too. Heather makes sure I like her perfume and is not interested in wearing anything that I am not attracted to. It is one of the unselfish things a wife can do for her husband rather than for herself.

Each morning, when we get up, Heather usually asks me what I would like her to wear that day. Rather than irritate her by saying, 'Wear what you like,' or 'I do not mind'; I usually ask what she has washed, ironed and ready and then make a choice. This is something I thoroughly enjoy doing.

However, if the outward adorning is all that there is to a wife, there is something seriously missing. The husband is the one who sees his wife when she wakes up dishevelled in the morning! He is not going to love her if she has nothing more to her than the outward show. The Bible says let there be more than that. If the husband is attracted to his wife by the holy and pure things that come out of her heart, he will not be disappointed whatever state he sees her in. Holiness is the foundation of beauty in a woman.

Honesty

Peter calls a gentle and quiet spirit an incorruptible ornament. Yet, many wives have an aggressive, critical spirit.

It is sad in counselling how many wives will freely talk about their husbands behind their backs. A husband is very blessed if he has an loyal and faithful wife in this respect. Set your heart to be a wife your husband will be proud of, even if he is not a Christian. That is real beauty, and is far more important than 'vital statistics'. The Amplified Version described this 'gentle and quiet spirit' as the 'Unfading charm of a gentle and peaceful spirit which (is not anxious or wrought up, but) is very precious in the sight of God'.

Such a one does not get anxious or ruffled when the children fall over. She is in control of her emotions. We are told the key in verse 5, that the holy women of old 'trusted in God'. Can you trust the Lord with your husband and children? One of the things that I am proudest about in Heather is that she is a woman who trusts God.

A prime example of this was during one of our camps, when Faith was only two and a half years old. Heather went to prepare a bath for her, leaving her to play with two teenage girls we knew, having already asked them to keep an eye on her. When Heather returned about two minutes later, the girls had disappeared and a voice from above said, 'Hello Mummy'. Faith had climbed on top of our two and a half ton van! Calmly, Heather said, 'Faith, come down,' and watched as she climbed down the same way that she had got up.

A Helpmeet

The Bible also says that a wife is a 'helpmeet' for her husband. That means she is to be supportive of him and never a hindrance. Suppose your husband loses his job, comes home and says, 'Darling, I have been made redundant'. Would you reply, 'Oh dear, you never could hold a job down. Whatever will we do about the mortgage?' How terrible! If your husband comes home having lost his job, be a helpmeet, build his faith by saying for example, 'I always knew you were worthy of a better job. We will just pray that you will have another one by next week. I believe in you.'

During a crisis a few years ago Heather was the voice of God to me and such an encouragement. Never would she allow a negative word or thought. She was behind me all the time. That is a helpmeet! Wives should be responsive to their husbands all the time, yet many fail here because they are so caught up with other things. Mothers tend to neglect their husbands, because they pay so much attention to the children. I am not saying that children do not need a lot of attention, (they certainly do) but it is important to remember that your first responsibility is towards your husband. He should still have the first place in your heart. Make sure that you set aside time every day to give him your undivided attention, not just in bed.

Romance

Both husbands and wives should continue to court their partner throughout their married life. You are a very special person, God made you to be romantic. If the desire for romance is missing from your life, then I believe you should go to God and ask him to sort out your emotions, so than you can be the romantic person He intends you to be. Many wives are lacking in this aspect, because there was never any romance in the home when they were young. However, it does not follow that because you have been married forty years and have never had any romance, or it has died, that you have missed your opportunity. God can put romance back into a marriage at any time.

When a husband finds affection in another woman, it is often because he didn't find it in his wife. I am not condoning a man running off with another woman; God will judge him for that. But often, it is not only his fault. Many a wife has driven her husband to that position, because she did not give him the romance he needed. If you sit on your husband's knee, there will not be room for the secretary!

Some wives seem to lose all interest in sex as time passes and no longer see it as having any significance in their marriage. They leave all the initiative to their husbands. However, it is good for the wife to take the initiative sometimes. Some wives go around the house saying 'hallelujah' all day and act like an ice-berg in bed. To their husband, their 'hallelujahs' are hollow and false, masking an attitude of coldness and indifference.

Constantly using the excuse of tiredness to opt out of sexual relationships is a real manifestation of selfishness. Selfishness in sexual relationship is sin. It can manifest itself in either being over demanding or unresponsive. Even if you have been overworking or doing those things you should not be doing and are 'too tired', is this loving your partner? Using sex to manipulate or bargain with your partner is sin too. Charismatic prayer meetings are so often a cop out for frustrated wives, frustrated because their marriage relationship is not right. So many Christians have a 'pseudo spiritual' attitude which leads to staleness in their marriage relationships. God made you as two human beings. He did not make you as angels to float around! He gave you each other to enjoy each other! If this is your problem:

Discuss it openly together.
Make a commitment to put it right, however long it takes.
Get some help, if necessary.

Food for Thought

Another way of showing love to your husband is to cook him his favourite meal. There are some wives who still do not know what their husband's favourite meals are! We are living in a fast food society. Do not give that to your husband, give of your best. He is the greatest gift God ever gave you outside of Jesus! There is an old saying that 'a way to a mans' heart is through his stomach.' I do not think that is entirely true, but it is very helpful. In some homes, if the husband is a little late, the food is thrown on to the plate anyhow, with the gravy running over the sides and stuck in the oven. When the poor man comes home after eight hours of hard work, it is then dumped in front of him with a 'There you are.' This is not the way to win him or keep him!

Seek to please your husband. Be the best wife possible. Have his meals ready when he gets home. There is nothing worse than seeing a wife peeling the spuds two minutes before her husband comes in through the door, because she has been out to some charismatic prayer meeting. Your husband is more important than prayer meetings! It is your God given ministry to care for him! Your husband and children are your top priority. Go to the prayer meetings by all means, but fit them into your schedule so that your husband's meals are ready when he comes in. When he arrives, meet him at the door. Be there with your arms wide open and tell him that you have missed him. Welcome him with the kind of kiss you would give him if he had been away for a month.

If you have to pack sandwiches for your husband, put a little love note in with them. I often find notes in my shirts when I unpack them on tour. Little things can mean such a lot. Make sure you keep his clothes nice, with all the buttons on his shirts and no holes in his socks. Keep your home spick and span and cook the meals as if you were cooking them for the Lord Jesus himself.

'Your reverence'

Finally, we are told that the wife is to reverence, honour and respect her husband. The Amplified version of Ephesians 5:33 is very interesting: 'Let each one of you (without exception) love his wife as (being in a sense) his very own self. Let the wife see that she respects and reverences her husband – that she notices him, regards him, honours him, prefers him, venerates and esteems him and that she defers to him, praises him, and loves and admires him exceedingly.'

I looked at the word 'reverence' in the Greek. It is only used this once in the entire Bible. God and your husband are the only ones who really qualify to be called 'Reverend'! Reverence, literally means to be 'terrified and affrighted'. Isn't that amazing! Yet this is the level of respect God expects a wife to give to her husband. It means to have your heart in submission to him and hold him in high esteem. Yet many wives are competing with their husbands. The hallmark of a Godly, sanctified woman is that she is in submission to her husband. Remember the chain of authority is God, Christ, husband, wife. The way you treat your husband goes up the chain to the Lord. The way you treat your husband is the way you are treating God.

Do you esteem your husband, honour him, prefer him, praise him, regard him exceedingly? Many Christian wives sit in the congregation looking at their pastors or other Christian men thinking, 'I wish I had a husband like him.' There is no man in all the world like your husband for you. God gave him to you! To be disrespectful of him is to be disrespectful to the God who gave him to you. I believe there is nothing more disrespectful than to hear a wife talking about her husband's faults to others.

Conclusion

Several years ago, a young woman heard me preach a message for wives. She left the meeting very angry and called me 'a male chauvinist pig.' Three years later I met her at another meeting and she fell into my arms and hugged me. She shared that she had only just got married at the time she heard me previously and was convinced that her way would work. After three years, when her marriage was falling apart and about to collapse, she remembered my words and acted on them. This had saved her marriage.

Male chauvinist pig or not (?), I follow the 'Maker's Instructions'. It works, put it to the test!

6. True Liberation

(Heather)

'And do no be conformed to this world but be transformed by the renewing of your mind, that you may prove what is that good and acceptable and perfect will of God.' (Romans 12:2)

This Scripure has a special significance for us as women. It is so easy to conform to the world's standards in the bringing up of our children or in our own relationship with our husbands, and not take the Bible as our standard. As the world seeks to influence us through the media and those around us, we need to turn more and more to the Maker's Instructions and discover the perfect will of God for us as women. We need to realize that a woman is not born a woman. Neither does she become one when she marries a man, bears his children and does his dirty linen or even joins a Women's Liberation Organisation. No, a woman becomes a woman in the true sense, when she begins to measure up to what God wants her to be. For any woman to be truly happy and fulfilled, it is necessary for her to see the plan God has for her. True happiness can only be found in Jesus Christ and in obeying His word. God makes us female, but we are trained to become a woman.

Women are looking for liberty and fulfilment, but as someone has rightly stated. 'Just as a room is not a room without walls, so liberty is not liberty without boundaries.' Our boundaries are the Word of God. Some women feel that, if they accept the Scriptures' teaching for wives, they will no longer have their own personality or standing. Happiness means fitting into God's plan. Woman is wonderfully made and designed by God to give pleasure. I believe that this is the whole principle of feminity. Woman was made to give pleasure, first of all to her man, and them to others including her children.

We are really liberated when we break free from competitiveness and jealousy. 'Woman's Lib' and 'Equal Rights for Women' advocates have caused a competitive spirit between male and females to such an extent, that it has become part of the 'norm', even in Church life. God never intended that there should be competitiveness between any human beings. One is really liberated when they break free from competitiveness and jealousy. Jesus gives us true freedom.

If we go back to the account of creation, we see that God, 'Created man in His own image, in the image of God created he him; male and female created He them.' (Genesis 1:27) It is as though God cut himself in two and put part of Himself in man and part of Himself in woman. In man he put certain characteristics, such as strength, protectiveness, and leadership, In woman he put tenderness, love of beauty, sensitivity etc. Together husband and wife can really complement one another and are thus better equipped to show forth the image of God.

Not Inferior

Adam was made first and then Eve, but because she came second that does not mean that she was inferior. Remember, Christ was referred to as 'the last Adam' and the 'second man', (1 Corinthians 15:45 and 47) Adam came first and Christ second but in that case the second was greater than the first. So woman is not inferior because she was made after man, but she is different! She was made to complement and complete the man. The Bible tells us that the woman is the glory of the man (1 Corinthians 11:7). If we can really see this and accept it, it will change our attitude to being a wife and mother.

In 1 Corinthians 11:3 we are given God's order, 'The head of every man is Christ and the head of the woman is the man and the head of Christ is God.' There are so many Christian women, especially single young ladies, who get uptight about the subject of submission and obedience.

Time to Adapt

Many women who get married say, 'I am going to be myself. I have always been like this; this is the way I intend to carry on.' I like the way that the Amplified version puts Ephesians 5:22, when it says, 'wives . . . . adapt yourselves to your own husband, as (a service) to the Lord.' If there is to be harmony, it is vital that you adapt yourself to your husband. As wives we are called to do the adjusting. This does not mean that our husbands are totally right or that they do not have to change. However, it is our responsibility to make sure that our part of the marriage relationship is working right. We need to look for areas in our lives where we can change and adapt, not pointing the finger at our husband, saying, 'If he changed, I would.' If we are truly going to be one, we must adapt to our partner's likes and dislikes. Many women marry with the idea that they are going to change their partner because they do not like this and that about him. But look at yourself and say, 'There are things about me which my partner may not like. I am going to adapt.' Then your marriage will become workable and real. If we can see that we are complementing our husbands, we will add to him and not take away. We are adding to the richness of man. We are going to bring out in him things which other people have not seen.

If you are married to a minister, and have not received a call yourself, then I challenge you to seek the Lord that you might receive one. You should be in the ministry together. I do not believe that the Lord would call a wife to a separate ministry, because God has made you one, and you should minister as one.

One of the most precious times in our marriage, was when Don and I, while facing a desperate issue in our lives, knelt at the communion rail in a church in County Durham where we were holding a crusade and dedicated ourselves to serving the Lord together. There we settled it, that the Lord and His call on our lives would come first in our relationship. We committed ourselves, whether together or apart, to doing the will of God, even if it meant at times, Don ministering away in the jungle, while I was at home with the family. Twenty-two years later, we look back on that day as the stabilising factor in our relationship. We never allow our overwhelming love for each other to interfere with the top priority, which is the call and gifting of God. On occasions I have had to strongly encourage Don to go off on a ministry trip when he has been reluctant to go without me, for we are both totally committed to the will and call of God on our lives.

True Submission

I cannot remember a time when I did not want to be in submission to Don. That does mean that I am a 'yes' person or that I voice no opinions. If I feel that he is making a wrong decision or taking a wrong course of action I take him aside and tell him so, but my submission means that having talked it through, I gladly do what he decides. I do not oppose him. In the English dictionary, the word 'submit' means to 'arrange your life under another's.' As wives we have to arrange our lives under those of our husbands.

If a woman submits in love to her husband, it will bring to the forefront all of his love. Hs will also begin to exercise his God-given authority and protective instincts. The once harsh husband can become strong and loving, because he no longer needs to be on the defensive to prove himself. Get right behind your husband and seek to make him a successful leader in every respect.

Some women say 'What do I sacrifice if I do not obey?' I believe we sacrifice protection. If we are obedient to authority, that is protection from pressure. God has ordained that we as women should have this protection, not only for our own sakes, but also for the testimony of Jesus Christ. We should desire to reflect the beauty of submission in our lives.

It does not make any difference how many years we have been married or who our husbands may be. We are to be in submission to our *own* husbands, and then, only then, do we come into the freedom and blessing which we yearn for in our marriage. Note, we are to be in submission to our husbands, not to the pastor or elders, our parents or anyone else, but to our husbands.

Time to Leave

> *'Therefore a man shall leave his father and mother and be joined to his wife, and they shall become one flesh.'* (Ephesians 5:31-33 and Genesis 2:24)

In marriage, a man and woman leave their parents' home to be joined as partners. That word 'leave' is vitally important, for many partners run back to their parents every five minutes, over every issue. You have started a new life together and in later years, when your children marry and leave home, take you hands off them. Just be there when they need you, so that they can come home for advice.

'As to the Lord.'

The Scriptures do not say submit to your husband if he is right. It is a command, an order from God. When we submit to our husband, we are not just submitting to a man: first of all we are submitting to God. The Scriptures tell us to submit, '*as to the Lord.*'

Submission is not gritting your teeth and saying, 'I have got to submit because God says so.' When submission is from the heart, it is easy. I believe that submission can become such an attitude in your heart that you do not realize that it is what you are doing. There is only one time when we are not to obey our husbands and that is if they ask us to do something which is in violation of God's Word. This is the only exception; every other time God requires us to submit. There have been times when Don has asked me to do something and I have not felt that it was right. I have said so, but have obeyed. Even when we submit feeling that the decision is wrong, God is always going to vindicate His Word and work the situation out for our good. Our submission is to the Lord, who rules, and because He rules, He can overrule in His own unique way if a husband should be wrong. With that kind of faith, we have confidence in our submission.

I heard someone comment that the Scripture teaches that the woman is an underdog or a slave. How can that possibly be? She can never be in an inferior role when she is in the place that God wants her to be.

Behind every successful marriage is a woman upholding and backing her man. The Lord will use the most ill-equipped husband to guide a submissive wife, simply because she stands behind delegated authority. A woman is secure under her husband's authority and may be more adventuresome than her sister who imagines herself without restraint.

A key to the matter of submission is trust. If you know that your husband loves you, you can freely submit, knowing that he has your interests at heart. A spiritually reticent man is often held back by his wife.

I believe that we should be united on every point and share with one another. Share your thoughts and the way you feel about an issue. At home, when I cannot reach Don and have to make a decision, I say to myself, 'Well, what would Don do?' If it is something which I am not sure about, I contact one of our group leaders or elders from the Church and ask for their covering for the decisions I make. It is essential too that you teach your family that your husband is the head of the home. If your children come and ask you something which is not your prerogative to make a decision on, channel them to your husband. I say to mine, 'Daddy's home now; go to him.'

There are times too, when you should tell your children that you need to be with your husband alone, and encourage them to go off and play. On no account, should children be allowed to come between you and your husband. This however, needs to be done sensitively, so as not to produce rejection in your children or a feeling of being unwanted. We need to take time to teach them how to be sensitive to other people's needs. One typical example is when their father comes home from work after a tiring day and needs time to relax and unwind.

The husband is the head of the home, but you are the one who has to create the atmosphere and it is up to you to create a good atmosphere for your family. Send your children to school with a happy image of Mummy. Wives, send your husbands to work with a happy image of you, so that they will have someone they want to come home to.

Home Truths

Let us now consider home. Wives should be 'discreet, chaste, homemakers, good, obedient to their husbands, that the Word of God may not be blasphemed' (Titus 2:5).

So often the world can point a finger at the Church because of what it sees in Christians' lives. We often bring dishonour and discredit to the Gospel because of the way we live. We should be, 'discreet, chaste, homemakers' so that our home may be glorifying to the Lord. I was brought up very strictly. Our family attended Church meetings three times on a Sunday and most nights of the week. Yet my mother kept the home clean and tidy, meals were always properly served and my father was always adequately cared for.

At 17, the Lord called me to serve him and I began travelling the country. When I started going into other Christian homes, I was shocked. I met some women who got up in the morning, and without making the beds and washing the dishes, went out all day to prayer meetings or visiting; and when the husband came home nothing had been done in the house. That, in my view, was dishonouring to the Gospel.

If I ever am at home and feel the Lord wants me to deal with a situation in the Church or team, I always give it to the Lord until I can get there. I do not accept the idea that God has told me to leave the washing up and visit Mrs So and So. God is big enough to keep the situation until I have fulfilled the duties in my home first.

See Jesus in your husband and family. After all, if your husband is saved, Jesus lives in Him. What would you do with your home if Jesus was going to live there? Well, he is there anyway, whether you consciously realize it or not. 'Whatever you do, no matter what it is, in word or deed, do all in the name of the Lord Jesus Christ, and in (dependence upon) His person, giving thanks to God the Father through Him.' (Colossians 3:17). We should cook meals, wash clothes, clean and tidy for our husbands, as unto Jesus. It makes a lot of difference if you see your so called daily 'mundane' tasks as being done unto the Lord and not doing them begrudgingly. Jesus said that, in as much as you do it unto one of the least of these, 'you do it unto me.' (Mathew 25:40) Suppose Jesus was coming to live with you. Are there things in your home you would want to change? Then change them, because He is living with you, all of the time, in your family, in your husband and in yourself.

Here are some practical applications we can make. Prepare a daily rota, jobs to be done by certain times. Have everything ready when your husband comes home. There is a saying, 'cleanliness is next to godliness.' There is no need for a Christian home ever to be dirty. Plan both a weekly and monthly rota.

Do things in an organized way. Have the children looking clean and tidy when your husband comes home. No father wants to cuddle and play with a grubby toddler. Keep the children so that he can be proud of them.

Redeemed from the Curse

As women we often find ourselves living in victory three weeks of every month and then the fourth week down we go – out for the count, defeated, depressed and dejected. It takes some of us the next week to regain victory, get free from condemnation and start again to be ourselves.

How many of us have considered that this is not what God planned for us? He never intended us to be like this. 'Men don't have to cope with what we do every month,' so many of us say. True – but they do have to cope with a wife or mother who is like this.

'Unto the woman he said, "I will greatly multiply your sorrow and your conception; in pain you shall bring forth children" (Genesis 3:16).

Here we have the beginning of all this suffering. Because of Adam and Eve's sin, God put a curse on her which down through the years all women have had to suffer. You may see this clearly but the understanding in itself does not remove the problems we have to face each month. Since 'Christ has redeemed us from the curse of the law' (Galatians 3:13), is it necessary to live in the shadow of someone else's sin? A study of Romans Chapters 4, 5, & 6 will give us a clearer picture of our redemption from the curse and the law. Adam sinned and we all fell! Jesus died that we may all live in victory over the results of Adam's sin.

Let us look at Genesis 3:16 in more detail. God said he would multiply your sorrow and your conception. To multiply you need a basis to start from, i.e. 2 x 2 = 4. Let us establish that there is a basis for our discomforts. Of necessity, there is the sensation of our seed producing itself and starting its course. There is some sensation, this is what has been greatly multiplied. Why? Because of sin.

This is the reason for all the symptoms so many of us experience. Depression, abnormal pain, water retention, imbalance of hormones, etc. etc. The good news is that we can be free from all these. We don't need healing, we need setting free from the effects of sin. We need to recognize fully what Jesus purchased for us on the cross. Many of us have experienced the benefits of this in part, examples are freedom from the power of sin, guilt, condemnation, healing and much more, but we still stay bound by Satan in this area, believing we have to suffer along with the rest of our families.

The same principle applies to the next part of our verse, 'In pain you shall bring forth children.' We need to see here again, that there is a basic pain one has to bear in giving birth to a child, but this has been multiplied by the effect of sin which entered the world when Adam and Eve rebelled. There is of necessity the contractions and the stretching of our bodies to bring the child to birth. But the intense pain and the complications which we have been taught by the world, our mothers, doctors and midwives to expect, are not what God planned when He made us. The Bible tells us that we shall be saved in childbirth if we 'continue in faith, love and holiness with self control' (Timothy 2:15). Notice this freedom is conditional upon us continuing in faith, love and holiness with self control. In other words, it is all tied up to our relationship with God. We do not annul God's Word by our past experience, but we should seek to make God's Word our present experience. God has made provision for us to live in victory in all parts of our life. He did this through the cross of Jesus Christ. It is here we must look for victory and deliverance from the curse.

My mother nearly lost her life when both my brother and I were born. She was in labour for two days with both of us. I was told that this would happen to me. So Don and I got down before the Lord and claimed God's promises in the Scriptures and have experienced complete freedom. In fact, some of the healthiest times of my life have been when expecting and bearing children.

Darling, I Love You

Now let us think a little about the subject of loving our husbands.

So many wives wonder why they are frustrated and I believe the answer lies here, at this point. God designed us that we need the release of a good marital relationship. Because the clock strikes bed-time, it does not mean now is the time to love your husband. You should have been loving him all day long, loving his good points and his bad, loving his ideas and his frustrations. Listening to him, to hear his plans and ideas about his job, complimenting him, touching his hand, ruffling his hair, showing him in little things that you love him. Then your relationship at night will be fulfilling and not just a 'duty'. Call him at the office and tell him that you love him.

Put a love note in his lunch box or in his case if he has to travel. Cook him his favourite meals. Experiment with different ways to express your love to him. Remember all the little ways you attracted him when you were courting. Do things that express your love for him.

As the years go by, romance is something which so often fades in marriages. This should not be so, rather is should grow, mature and become more precious. Remember the little things that used to be so special and how they have gone out of your experience ans seek to reinstate them.

Problems sometimes arise from partners wanting to make love at different times of the day. For example, one partner may prefer love making at night, while the other favours the morning when feeling refreshed from a good night's sleep. These things present an opportunity for consideration and showing unselfish love. For, *'The wife does not have authority over her own body, but the husband does. And likewise the husband does not have authority over his own body, but the wife does. Do not deprive one another except with consent for a time, that you may give yourselves to fasting and prayer; and come together again so that Satan does not tempt you because of your lack of self control.'* (1 Corinthians 7:4 & 5.)

A legalistic response to this Scripture, of having intercourse out of a sense of duty, is not enough. There needs to be a loving response from the heart, which God can supply, even though for one reason or another you might prefer not to. If you deprive your husband in the realm of your sexual relationship, you are causing him to be tempted. When a husband has extra marital relationships, it is often to a great extent, the wife's fault. You have a responsibility before God for your husband to see that he is sexually fulfilled.

Always find time to listen to your husband and to hear his plans and ideas about his job, It is your responsibility to complement him. You should be the first one, next to God, that your husband comes to. Some men have extramarital relationships because their wives will not listen to them. They leave home in the morning, perhaps, with their wives sitting at the breakfast table, drinking black coffee with curlers in their hair and the home untidy. They go to a job where everything is organised, with a very efficient secretary, who dresses smartly, and what do they see in their mind? The way they left their wives. What do they expect to get when they arrive home in the evening. Someone looking untidy and at the end of her tether? Organize yourself for when he comes home. Do not welcome him home in the clothes you have worked in all day, but smarten yourself up, and tidy your hair. If he is on shift work at irregular hours, it is so important that you adapt yourself to be ready for him.

Dressed for the Occasion

'Also (I desire) that the woman should adorn themselves modestly and appropriately and sensibly in seemly apparel, not with elaborate hair arrangement or gold or pearls or

expensive clothing.' (1 Timothy 2: 9 & 10. Amplified Bible)

In this Scripture we read of a woman's outward appearance, how God desires us to look. We should dress:
a) *Modestly* The Oxford dictionary defines this as being inconspicuous. I believe that includes not being flamboyant, loud or common but modestly dressed and glorifying to God.
b) *Appropriately* For example, if you were going for a country walk on a farm, if would be inappropriate to wear an evening blouse, full length dress and lots of jewellery. If you were to be presented to the Queen it would not be appropriate for you to wear a dirty old pair of jeans. To dress appropriately means to wear clothes that suit the occasions.
c) *Sensibly* Wear 'seemly apparel'. This I feel, includes not wearing extremely short skirts and low-cut dresses but dressing to glorify God.

As I travel around the country, meeting hundreds of Christian women, so often their untidiness is apparent.

I believe that the God whom I represent is worthy of my best. My husband and family, whom I love are also worthy of my best.

No husband, parent, or child wishes to be associated with someone unkempt or careless in appearance.

Young ladies need teaching to be real ladies. Femininity is one attribute of a Christian woman which has been lost in today's society. The Old Testament tells us, 'A woman shall not wear anything that pertains to a man, nor shall man put on a woman's garment, for all who do so are an abomination to the Lord your God' (Deuteronomy 22:5). I remember as a teenager seeing a woman I knew quite well, who dressed as a man. She wore a man's suit, socks and shoes. Everything about her was manly. Her whole attitude was that of a man. This is what God was talking about. We should be able to tell at a glance who is a man and who is a woman. Our young ladies should be taught that they do not go to a man's shop to buy their clothes, and if they go to a unisex shop, they should be careful to buy only clothes that are feminine.

Many courting and engaged couples say, 'What shall I wear?' It is a good idea for couples to go out and buy their clothes together to please each other. This way they will not have a wardrobe full of clothes which their partner does not like. I do not think we should tell our young people that they should not follow the fashions of today, providing the latest fashion is not an immodest one. They can use the fashions and be fashionably dressed, yet still be godly men and women. How we dress expresses the attitude of our heart, therefore if our heart is truly righteous towards God, that will be expressed in the way we dress.

How many of you see areas of weakness in your life as a wife? I would challenge you to deal with those weaknesses. The result will be happiness greater than you ever thought possible and the smile and blessing of God on your home.

Ten Commandments for Wives

1. Thou shalt love the Lord thy God with all thy heart, mind, soul and strength and your husband only a little less than you love God (Deut 6:5).
2. Thou shalt gladly submit to thy husband, as unto the Lord (Eph 5:22).
3. Thou shalt keep thy tongue with all diligence, being careful to bless and encourage your husband verbally at least once a day and never to discuss openly with others intimate details about your love relationships (Prov. 31:26, 11:16).
4. Thou shalt keep a joyful heart in all that your daily schedule calls upon you to do. (Col 3:17).
5. Thou shalt put far from thee a jealous or selfish nature (Prov 6:34).
6. Thou shalt give diligence to keep thyself and thy home attractive, remembering thou must not only win thy husband's love but also keep it. (Prov 31:27, 28).

7. Thou shalt greatly prefer thy husband, never comparing him unfavourably with other men. Sincerely admire and honour him (Eph. 5:33).
8. Thou shalt prize thy womanly virtues and value them more than life itself (Prov 12:4).
9. Thou shalt instill in thy children a love, respect and devotion for their father. (Prov. 22:6)
10. Thou shalt not nag. (Prov 25:24, & 27:15).

7. Which One?

A couple were once overheard to say, 'When we got married we were told that we now became one. Ever since then, we have been arguing about which of us is the one.'

God wants a husband and wife to be whole as a couple. He wants us to be one. God who is a triune being, Father, Son and Holy Spirit, made us in His image. He made us triune beings, body, soul and spirit. For us to be whole, we have to be whole in each of these areas, and for us to be whole as couples we have to be rightly related to each other in body, soul and spirit.

One in Body

When a couple marry and relate together physically they become one flesh. This is very natural, and God wants us to enjoy our sexual relationship. Any idea to the contrary, regarding sex to be something evil, unclean or unnecessary is of the devil. God created the sexual relationship. He made it so that we could multiply and have children, but He also made it to be enjoyed.

One in the Spirit

When both partners are saved and baptized in the Holy Spirit, they become one spirit. I often tell couples to seek God to become one in Spirit before they are joined together in the flesh. One of the problems in marriages is that the couple are often unequally yoked. Some consider this to just mean a Christian married to a non-Christian. This, of course, is bound to cause problems. However, I believe that 'unequally yoked' applies equally when one partner is baptized in the Holy Spirit and the other is not.

A couple should be able to pray together, worship together, and serve together in every aspect of their lives. Heather and I are one in spirit.

At a conference some while ago, the men were with me, and the women were in another room with Heather. We had all been given a portion of Scripture and asked to meditate on it for ten to fifteen minutes, expecting God to show us things from His Word, We were not allowed to include anything we had heard or seen before, but had to believe God for something new.

It was a marvellous time. The Lord showed me things I had never seen before, even to the extent that I was a little concerned because I thought it might seem to be controversial. When we went to the breakfast table, I shared these thoughts with Heather. She said, 'That's wonderful. God showed me exactly the same thing. I was the only one who had this, and the others were really blessed by it.' I believe that illustrates one of the goals that God wants a husband and wife to have – to be one in spirit so that they have the same revelation from God.

Once when I was in Chile God shared something with me, so I wrote home and shared it with Heather. By the time she got the letter, she had already written to me saying the very same thing. God had already spoken to her about it, although we were several thousand miles apart.

There is a place of oneness in spirit where, as far as the things of God are concerned, you can move together. I never entertain the idea that Heather and I are anything elso but one in spirit. We never consider ourselves as two individuals. We have different personalities but God has put us together to make us one whole.

One in Soul

Have you noticed how a husband and wife can be flowing in the Spirit together during the Sunday morning service?

For example, the husband brings a message in tongues and the wife gives the interpretation. Yet an hour later they have begun to grate on each other, leading to arguments and anger over a mundane thing like getting the lunch ready. How can this be? The fact is, they have never learned to relate where it really counts. Building takes place in the soul realm. In Acts 4:32, we are told that the Church were 'of one heart and one soul and with great power gave the apostles' witness to the resurrection of the Lord Jesus.' What was the key to their effectiveness? It was not just because they were of one heart but also because they were of one soul too! They had learnt to relate soul to soul. Many marriages are in trouble because the partners have never learnt to relate soul to soul.

In the soul there is the will, the mind and the emotions. Until we are willing to open up our lives and be built together in these areas we will never be truly one. Some couples live together for sixty or more years and even die, having never become truly one.

The will

Have you ever said of your partner, 'They have a will of their own'? Well, that statement is true, but God wants us to become one in our will. This is never arrived at easily or painlessly, but it is possible.

Heather loves history, which naturally I do not find enjoyment in at all. I love nature. It is not difficult to see how a disagreement could arise. 'I want to see the deer'. 'Well I want to see the castle'. There needs to be a mutual submission in our hearts. Selfishness is responsible for such matrimonial disharmony. When my heart is right, I can do things which I would not choose to do, because I want to please Heather. What is more, I go to enjoy myself, not to put up with it, and I look for things to enjoy.

It is possible for a couple to be one in will. I used to hate going shopping. Now I love it and I do not like Heather to go without me, because God has changed me. I used to feel like a little dog on a lead, looking in the windows, 'Do you like this one, do you like that one?' But it has all changed because I opened my heart, and asked God to change me.

What do we do when two strong wills are involved?

Anyone who knows Heather and I, know that we both have strong wills. The only answer to a strong will is submission. We are told in Ephesians 5:21 'Submit yourselves to another.' Our submission is not really tested until we disagree. The word 'submit' means to 'arrange your life under'. Submission is not imposed dictatorship that comes from the top. It starts with an arranging of your life under that of another. There is a place here where the husband also needs to submit to his wife. Mutual submission is a key to becoming one in will.

Look at Jesus. When He was in the Garden of Gethsemane, He showed us the perfect way. He prayed, 'Father, if it be possible, let this cup pass from me. Nevertheless, not my will, but thine be done.' (Matt. 26:39). This shows us that the Son in His humanity, had a will separate from His Father's will. He said, 'If it be possible, let this cup pass from me.' (That is His humanity). 'Nevertheless, *not my will* but yours be done.'

That is how Jesus lived. The Bible tells us that He did not do anything unless His Father showed Him. This teaches us how our wills should be. He never once had His own way. If He had, in independence of His Father, we could never have been redeemed. That is how serious it is. In everything He submitted to His Father's will.

We see the depth of this truth in Jesus' words, as translated in the Amplified Bible, 'I am able to do nothing from myself independently, of my own accord; but as I am taught by God and as I get His orders. (I decide as I am bidden to decide. As the voice comes to me, so I give a decision) Even as I hear, I judge and my judgement is right (just, righteous) because I do not seek or consult my own will – I have no desire to do what is pleasing to myself, my own aim, my own purpose – but only the will and pleasure of the Father who sent me' (John 5:30).

'Christ did not please Himself.' (Rom. 15:3) That should be the goal in our relationships together. We have to come to the place where we lay our wills down and allow God have His way.

The mind

Education, theology and our upbringing have shaped our thinking. So, often, when two minds get together they think differently and BOOM! There is an explosion!

Our minds have to be renewed. When we recognize that it is God who has called us together as one and commit ourselves to becoming all that He wants us to be, we will both begin to hear Him saying the same thing. This is not uniformity but harmony.

What is more, one will complement the other. What she has is mine and what I have is hers. Heather is academically good, but due to tuberculosis in my formative years I missed a great deal of schooling. However, because we are one, I do not feel inferior, nor does Heather feel superior. Together there is a beautiful harmony. What Heather has, she has given to me. When she said in our marriage vows 'With all my worldly goods I thee endow,' she gave herself to me. She gave her educated mind to me, so her gift is mine and we work together. I do not feel a failure in this area, together we are one. I can work out the contents of a letter, but she can do the writing and spelling. (When I am away and write to Heather she needs the gift of interpretation to understand it! (Paper-work jobs which would take her a couple of days would take me all year! Yet together there is a complementing and efficiency.

The emotions

Finally, there is the realm of the emotions. Many Christians hold some extremely strange ideas about emotions. They say, 'You must not be emotional when you go to Church.' That means I leave my soul behind! The Bible tells us the elders have to watch over our 'souls' (Heb 13:17), so if I leave mine at home, it would be very difficult for them! The Bible teaches that wherever my soul goes, my emotions are involved. I cannot think of anyone more emotional than the woman who washed Jesus' feet with her tears and dried them with her hair.

A lot of couples cannot weep together or laugh together. The Lord wants to melt our hearts so that we can weep in His presence. Jesus was touched with the feelings of our infirmities. We also need to be able to be touched with one another's infirmities. Very often one partner cannot feel how the other feels because of a hard heart. We need to get before the Lord so that He can soften it. He gave us our emotions. Tears are very precious to the Lord. Rather than condemn the woman who washed His feet with her tears, Jesus said, 'Leave her alone. Wherever the Gospel is preached, this event will be remembered.' For our lives to be built together, we have to become one in the emotional realm too.

It is vital that we are totally open with each other and come to the place where we can truly share our hearts. Perfect love casts out fear, so if there is love between us, we are not going to be threatened by one another. I will be able to say anything that needs to be said without threatening my partner. There will be no need to wear a mask, pretending to be what we are not. If we really love each other, we will trust one another and lay down our lives for each other.

If someone is one degree under, it affects the way they react. Therefore, we need to let our partner into our lives, so that they will know how we really feel, otherwise they will be frustrated.

Emotional hang-ups

We are all different emotionally. So we need to take time to understand our partners emotions. Together we can blend to make a whole. This is very different from seeking to be carbon copies of each other. However, although we are all different emotionally, I do not believe that one person should have to be dominant in the love making. Yet many feel bottled up and unable to express themselves. We are made in the image of God who is certainly not stifled or unable to express Himself and this is how he wants us to be. Let us consider four major causes of this emotional stifling:-

1. Childhood hurts. Many children wanted love, but were pushed aside by their mother or father. This has caused a fear of expressing themselves in case they get hurt again. One manifestation of this hurt is that, one or both partners relate together in sexual lust, rather than genuine love. The sex act is really wanted for self gratification, rather than as an opportunity to give. Of course, down the road there are many problems, because lust never lasts. The answer is to come before the Lord (getting help if necessary) so that He can heal those hurts.

2. Ignorance. In marriage counselling, it is amazing how frequently we discover that a lack of affection between a husband and wife goes back to a childhood, where their parents did not show affection for each other. Many children never saw their parents express any physical affection in front of them. So even up to adulthood they saw any expression of emotion in love, as a thing to be suppressed and not expressed. It is vital that parents are free in front of their children, showing affection to be normal and wholesome.

3. Cultural background. 'British reserve' is both ungodly and anti-biblical. I encourage you to read the Song of Solomon in the light of it being an account of two lovers expressing themselves to each other. I believe that this itself should release you into a new dimension. Express yourself emotionally and thus become one with your partner.

4. Guilt complex. Brian and Christine were in their early twenties and had been going out together (on and off) for five years. I knew them both very well and had a real heart for them. One night I noticed how defeated and disheartened Christine looked. I went to her after the meeting to find out what was wrong to be told bluntly, 'Nothing.' I looked her in the eyes and said, 'You know me better than to give an answer like that'. At which point it all came out. They had broken up, (yet again). When I asked why, she explained that they couldn't cope sexually, and had gone further than they should again.

To my question as to whether they felt they were right for each other, she affirmed that they definitely did, and loved each other very much. But because of their strong sexual desires for each other, they thought it must be wrong. I replied that it was perfectly normal for two human beings in a boy/girl relationship to feel this way for each other and that I would be worried if they didn't! I said, rather than call it off, I felt they should marry. As Paul said, 'It is better to marry than burn with passion.' (1 Cor. 7:9).

She left with a new release and after talking it through with Brian, they were engaged within a month and a year later they were married. Guilt makes a person unable to discern a healthy desire and then to practise self-control. Pre-marital or extra-marital sex, homosexuality or lesbianism cause a guilt complex which can so emotionally stifle a person that they cannot express themselves properly.

So many marriage problems are caused by guilt from past sin, which has been suppressed and hidden from the person's partner. It is vital to repent and come into the light with your partner, ideally before you marry; but, if you have not, be very sensitive and prayerful so as not to drop your confession on your partner suddenly.

All extra marital sex is sin. If a couple committed fornication before they married or even with someone else before meeting their partner, it can affect their whole marriage, trust and mental attitude, not just their sex life. It often manifests itself many years later. Because all fornication is sin, even if the couple eventually marry, it needs to be truly repented of and prayed about for the power of the cross to eradicate all effects.

It is possible to be one in mind, will and emotions, but it will require a mutual submission to each other. There may also be wrong thoughts, desires, and emotional responses which need to be repented of, so that the Lord can deal with them in our hearts. Building soul to soul should be the priority with your partner, but is so important with other members of your family and also with brothers and sisters in the church too. What testimony is it to the world when they see Christians criticizing, backbiting, and losing their temper? As we have seen, it is in the soul realm where the grating takes place. With almost everyone I have sought to build with soul to soul, it has not been pleasant to start with. It has been painful. Yet it is so vital. Are you prepared for God to build your life soul to soul with your partner?

8. No Entry

It does not matter how long a couple have known each other before they marry, until they begin to live and share their lives together, they are really still strangers. However, as we have seen it is possible to live together and raise children, yet still remain two isolated individuals. I have met some couples who have been together thirty or forty years, yet they still do not *really* know each other. Now is the time for a couple to begin to build in depth and really get to know each other, to thoroughly enjoy one another's company and long to do things together. Then retirement will be something to look forward to, because they have already learned to spend their time together. Otherwise, when the children leave home, there will be two elderly people, living in the same house, but lonely.

Loneliness is the fruit of a lack of a deep relationship with anyone. We see it expressed in Jesus' words from the cross, 'My God, my God, why have you forsaken me?' (Mathew 15:34) It is probably the most painful and hurtful thing a person can ever suffer.

One vital key is the willingness to open our hearts and come to the place where we have no secrets from each other and there are no 'no go' areas.

For the first ten years of our marriage, Heather and I were fearful of each other's reactions if certain subjects arose. These subjects were avoided and they become 'no go' areas.

We did not realize that these fears were the result of hurts and rejections in our lives, from which we needed ministry to be set free. They caused a bondage which made us react badly, because we were always looking for acceptance. The more acceptance we got, the more we needed, because you can never be satisfied while the bondage of rejection is there. Praise God, we now know that we are accepted in the beloved and it is this love that has set us free to love each other and deepen our relationship with Christ and one another.

It was a long while before I let Heather into the secrets of my heart. I regret the delay now. We need to allow our partner entry to our innermost secrets so that they get to know who we really are. Nobody wants to relate to an external veneer. This only leads to frustration in our marriage. A veneer simply covers up the real thing. We need to learn to communicate in reality. How often do we say things that are just on the surface?

One night, while driving together to a meeting I was speaking at, Heather and I found the strength to begin to open up. It was one of the greatest days of our marriage.

A part truth

So often we share only the 'successes' in our lives and conceal the things which would be regarded as failure. It is pride which causes us to seek to build up a 'total success' image for our partner. God warns us that 'Pride goes before destruction' (Prov. 16:18). 'Only by pride does contention come' (Prov. 13:10) So, where there is contention in a relationship, the cause is pride.

We need to openly talk through our fears, our desires and the problems we face. To share the things that hurt inside. I want to really know the things that hurt Heather and she wants to know what hurts me.

So often it seems easier to settle for 'peace at any cost' . . . but it is a false peace and never lasting. It is like sitting on the edge of a volcano that is about to erupt. Commit yourselves, long before the arguments or problems arise, that you will 'speak the truth in love'. For, 'Can two walk together unless they are agreed?' (Amos 3:3).

I used to frustrate Heather by hiding from her how I really felt when I was unwell. I almost regarded it as a sin to acknowledge anything negative and therefore felt unable to tell her. I actually thought that this 'pseudo spiritual' reaction was godly! It was so ingrained in my lifestyle, Heather had to get Mike Darwood, one of my fellow Elders, in to help her communicate this to me. In reality, I was keeping her out of my life. What a relief it was to be able to share things in honesty so that we could stand together. The devil did not stand a chance. It also brought a new depth into our love for each other, for, 'Though one may be overpowered by another, two can withstand him. And a threefold cord is not quickly broken.' (Eccles. 4:12) The strong are called to support the weak. (Acts 20:35)

The Pain Barrier

Some couples find in trying to open up and build together that one or the other reacts wrongly, thus preventing issues being faced and worked through. Someone aptly described this as the 'Pain Barrier.' Couples need to get to the place where they are *both* committed to going through the Pain Barrier, otherwise we are never going to know victory in that area. If this really seems impossible, the answer is to find another couple whom you can both trust to share with, so that they can help you through. Sharing your failures and the secrets of your hearts will require a real commitment.

Ouch!

Past hurts and rejection stop many people communicating and responding rightly. God wants to heal those hurts. Some react in a heated moment with statements like 'You're hopeless' or 'I wish I'd never married you.' These are like weeds sown into a person's heart and can do untold damage, that continues long after they were said.

It is not possible to build a strong relationship of the deepest sort with someone who is hurt unless you are together prepared to recognize that hurt and seek the Lord's healing from them. Time does not heal, it merely buries an issue. The problem is still there in the subconscious, as reactions will amply demonstrate. Only a genuine openness, love and forgiveness can bring healing.

Defenceless

One of the first things my mother-in-law said to me was, 'Don, we can never win with you, because you are always willing to be wrong.' I certainly seek to be and wish I 'always' was. This kind of openness is so important if we are going to be honest with one another. The Lord is the only one who is always right! We need to repent of any proud, 'I am right, you are wrong' attitude, as it will ruin a relationship. Another manifestation of the same attitude is the statement; 'It's always me that is wrong.' Which is really saying, 'I am always right.' Stubborness is sin, and a great hindrance to building relationships.

Our Problems

If we really believe that we are one, we will see that any problems our partner may have is not 'his' or 'her' problem but 'our' problem.

Until we are right on this point, we will confront the person and not the issue and nothing will change. It does not matter so much who the issue concerns. We are 'one' and should face the issue together. It is against us! This makes us more vulnerable, as it may well be our actions which causes our partner's bad response in the first place. When necessary, be quick to apologize and to ask forgiveness.

We need to see that it is not our job to bring about change in our partner. We are called to accept them as they are, in the same way that Christ accepted us. Have you ever seriously considered what you were like when Christ accepted you? I was rotten through and through. God says, 'Now accept one another.' Husbands, accept your wives. Wives accept your husbands with all their faults and weaknesses. You will find that in the very act of true acceptance, strength will begin to come in those areas. When this attitude is right, we can soberly confront any issues. The time to do this is not in the midst of an issue, but at an unemotoional moment. There is often a temptation to express hurt or anger with accusations, shouting or hard words. However, such actions are destined to failure. The Bible tells us that, 'A gentle answer turns away wrath, But a harsh word stirs up anger' (Prov. 15:1)

Such terms as, 'You never . . . .' or 'You always . . . .' are an attack, therefore the usual response is for the accused to go on the defensive or throw back an equally hard rebuttal. Accusations seldom bring the desired results. They usually increase the hostility. Use of the term, 'I feel . . .' can play an important part in effective communication. For example, 'I feel left out and ignored. I may be wrong, but that is how I feel.' It is also important to guard the volume level. When my wife approaches me with a sincere expression of her feelings, rather than feel threatened, I am prompted to respond sensitively and discuss the matter in a constuctive way.

Relationships – never on the line

We need to know that our partner loves us enough not to reject us. Heather and I are secure in this love. I know whatever she found out about me, she would not reject me. She knows too, that whatever I found out about her, I would not reject her. Our relationship is never on the line. Therefore, we can honestly face issues, knowing that they will never part us. We are committed to working out any problems we may face. This security and trust has to be built.

In the early days of a marriage, there are very few

couples who really know this security. It comes out of building our lives together and is strengthened as our love for one another is tested. When the Lord tries our faith we come forth as pure gold. The same thing happens when our love is tried through the problems we face in our marriage. We need to openly show and confess our loyalty for each other. If you have ever been guilty of threatening to leave when things were not going your way, stop playing that childish game. Make a commitment to your partner now, that from today your relationship will never again be on the line but that you will be loyal to each other at all times.

Some Christians live in fear that they have married the wrong partner. It is the devil who would encourage this fear. The moment we marry and our marriage is consummated, we become one and His will is for us to stay as one. So, you can face any issues knowing that your relationship is not at stake. As far as God is concerned, there is no such thing as incompatability. God has given us His grace to work out our relationships.

What's that you said?

Probably 99% of marriage problems are caused by bad communications. We are so often vague and superficial. There is no depth of love in vagueness. We need to 'tell it like it is'. Communication is a vital key to successful relationships. Yet it is a key few of us have learned how to use because so much of our lives remain locked up, undisclosed and undiscovered by each other.

Learn to react positively when your partner asks what you would like to do. 'I don't mind. I'll do whatever you want to do' is usually a cop out and makes no contribution to the relationship. Be real and say what is in your heart, even if you add 'If there is something you would rather do, I would be happy.'

So often a wife does not know what her husband wants her to become and vice versa. Again, this takes a great openness in our hearts to share. I want Heather to know what I want her to be, what my desires for her are and I want to know her desires for me.

Discover your partner's desires and the things that motivate them. What is it that makes them angry, hurt or happy and what are their likes and dislikes? One of the practical results of this discovery, was that my dirty linen now goes into a basket rather than into a pile on the floor. I often recommend that couples write each other an honest and frank letter sharing:

something that they love most about their partner.
something that they most want to receive from them.
something that irritates them the most.

Doing this has been very effective in improving lines of communication. At a recent married couples weekend where we did this, one wife testified that it was the first letter she had received from her husband in twenty one years. It had done their marriage wonders. I suggest that you could both do this now.

9. Love and Forgiveness

'When you stand praying, forgive, if you have ought against any; that your father also which is in heaven may forgive you your trespasses. But if you do not forgive, neither will your father which is in heaven forgive your trespasses.' (Mathew 11:23-26)

At the end of one of our missions in Northamptonshire, I was on an 'any questions' panel with a vicar who had been involved in the crusade. We had been sharing the Gospel there clear and straight for three weeks. So, when one of the questions came up, 'You have preached that no matter how seriously we have sinned, if we come to the Lord Jesus, repent of our sins, ask Him to forgive us and cleanse us in His precious blood and receive Him into our hearts and lives, we will be forgiven. Is that right?' You can imagine how thrilled we were and eager to seize the opportunity to preach the Gospel to the congregation there. After we had finished, it came to the vicar's turn, a dear elderly gentleman and a wise man. This is what he said, 'I agree with all my evangelist friends have said, but there is one further thing. There is an extra condition and that is that you forgive. For the Bible says, *'If you do not forgive, neither will your Father who is in heaven forgive your trespasses.'* That made quite an impact on me, and brought over in a new way how serious it is to hold grudges against anyone.

So many people's lives are one constant round of problems, the root of cause being resentment. Depression is often caused because deep down inside there is a hurt or grudge against someone. While a person is in that condition, his Christianity just cannot work. Yet it is amazing how many of these people want a short cut to victory. They come seeking prayer and get a measure of victory, but do not understand why their problems come back again. You cannot build a by-pass around resentment and leave the unforgiving attitude inside, hoping that it will go away. It has to be faced, fairly and squarely.

The greatest love words

'I forgive you', are the greatest love words that can ever be spoken. In fact, I believe they are stronger than the words, 'I love you'. Forgiveness is the cement that keeps families together. Picture the Lord dying on the cross, His back bleeding where it had been whipped, nails through his hands and feet, a crown of thorns on His head, His face raw where they had plucked out His beard, while the people stood mocking Him and soldiers offered Him vinegar to drink. Yet he prayed, *'Father, forgive them, for they, do not know what they do'* (Luke 23:34). To me those are the greatest words of love that have ever been spoken in the universe. Love is far more than what I call the 'sloppy, sentimental slush' presented to us on our television screens. Consider the impact of those words, 'Father forgive them, for they do not know what they do', as the people who had hammered in those nails and plucked out his beard stood around. He wanted them forgiven.

We cannot love in this way in our own strength. However, the Bible tells us 'The Love of God has been poured out in our hearts by the Holy Spirit who was given to us'. (Romans 5:5). God's love is given to us to that we can forgive as He forgave and obey Jesus' commanded to 'love your enemies'. (Matt. 5:44). Jesus did not say that we will never have enemies, but that when we do we are to love them. As a preacher once put it we are to 'love them to death.' In other words, love them until they no longer exist as an enemy, for 'love never fails'. It is a wonderful thing to be able to love those who deliberately set out to hurt us and to be able to truly forgive them.

During my early Christian days I went through an experience which was so cruel that I found myself in a position where I could have committed murder, according to the laws of this land, and got away with it. Yet at that moment, God filled my heart with His love and grace. I walked over to this person and put my arms around him, I kissed him and said, 'I love you'. I do not know what that did for him, but it certainly did something for me. I could have built up a whole condition of hatred and resentment that would have been catastrophic to my health, apart from anything else, but God enabled me to forgive.

It is no good turning around and blaming the people we resent, even if it is 100% their fault. You can still forgive them and love them. In fact, it is your responsibility before God to love them and forgive them. The Bible tells us, 'If your enemy hungers, feed him; if he thirsts give him a drink; for in so doing you will heap coals of fire on his head. Do not be overcome by evil, but overcome evil with good' (Romans 12:20). We are to bless those who curse us and be good to those who despitefully use us. God does not tell us to do anything which we are not able to do and which he will not give us the grace to carry through.

How many times?

Peter wanted to be right on forgiveness. It was an area that he was not quite sure about, so he said to the Lord, 'How often shall my brother sin against me and how many times do I have to forgive him? Up to seven times?' The Lord replied, 'I do not say to you, up to seven times but up to seventy times seven' (Matt. 18:22). Mathematicians can work out how many times that is, but I tell you, if you try forgiving someone that many times, by the time you have forgiven them, you will have forgotten the number of times you have forgiven them, so you will just go on forgiving! Think of Peter and the messes and failure that he got himself into, yet he was the man that on the day of Pentecost was so greatly used of God.

Receiving forgiveness

Many people find it hard to receive forgiveness. They sin against another person, who forgives them, but somehow they cannot forgive themselves. They live in a constant realm of condemnation, which saps their spiritual life and sometimes destroys them. We need to see that it is an issue of pride, if you cannot forgive yourself. The Bible says, 'God resists the proud, but gives grace to the humble' (James 4:6).

Loving as Jesus loved means that however much we have been used or hurt, we find a place of forgiveness.

Paul expressed a wonderful attitude when he said to the Church at Corinth, 'To whom you forgive anything, I also forgive; for if indeed I have forgiven anything, I have forgiven that one for your sakes in the presence of Christ' (2 Cor. 2:10). I get lots of letters from folks who say, 'Will you forgive me?' For the majority I never even knew that they had done anything wrong. However, they are people who want to be right. You will never progress with God until this issue of forgiveness is dealt with. Before Paul knew they needed forgiveness he had forgiven them. Paul was concerned about keeping himself clean and right before God.

Many people have a chip on their shoulder. Sometimes it is because they feel that their parents have failed them or let them down. Others were orphaned and feel that life has dealt them a cruel blow. Deep down inside, if the secrets of their hearts were revealed, they would be blaming God for it. Others have a hang up because they are illegitimate. Jesus knows how you feel and He can identify with you and bring you to the place where you are completely released from all these hang-ups so that you can forgive. Have you ever considered this? The Lord was born of the Virgin Mary, the Holy Spirit being His Father, yet Joseph accepted Him as his own son. Because of this Jesus was accused of being illegitimate. What is more, both Joseph and Mary had illegitimacy in their lineage, according to the Scriptures.

Jesus can identify with you and wants to heal the hurt in your heart, so that you can forgive and forget. What I mean by forgetting is not that you can never think about the occasion again, but that the sting is taken out of it so that it no longer affects you. Then you will no longer hold anything against those involved but you will be able to look them right in the eyes and truthfully say, 'I love you and forgive you.'

Forgiveness – key to a healthy life

Forgiveness is a key to health. So much disease comes from the basic root of unforgiveness. It is a fact that one form of arthritis is caused from bitterness and resentment, which dries up the flow of fluid in the joints. However, far more damage is done on the spiritual side through resentment.

We need to learn to forgive the people who do not agree with us. To forgive the church down the road which does not have the same doctrines as you. Maybe there are people in your own church whom you need to forgive. We go to some churches where we find folks who haven't spoken to each other for twenty years. Is it any wonder that most of the pews are empty? The Bible says, 'For he who does not love his brother who he can see, how can he love God whom he has not seen' (1 John 4:20).

To say that you are right with God when you are not right with your mother, father, minister or anyone else is a contradiction. So often, when young people become Christians and their parents are not saved, it leads to all kinds of tensions in the home. This calls for forgiving them, loving them and serving them. You will never win them by being contentious!

Maybe there are those with you now whom you need to forgive or to ask forgiveness from. Or maybe you need to phone someone or make a point of asking their forgiveness the next time you are with them.

The family – a perfect opportunity

In the family, there will be plenty of opportunity to forgive. Husbands, as head of your family, it is your responsibility to initiate forgiveness, even if your wife is 100% at fault, (which is very unlikely). For we are to love our wives as Christ loved the Church, when He gave himself for it. On the cross, Jesus was totally right and mankind was totally wrong, yet the Lord initiated forgiveness. Do not allow long periods to pass without forgiving. Take a lead in asking forgiveness too. It might be painful, but it takes the sting out of the situation and keeps love flowing. So get in quick! Seeking to hold out for as long as possible is the result of pride and is a recipe for disaster. The very essence of love is forgiveness.

Bed is not the place to be reconciled. If there is a problem, it should be dealt with that day. The Bible tells us 'Do not let the sun go down on your wrath' (Eph. 4:26).

Where necessary, take a lead in apologizing and asking forgiveness. It may hurt your pride. After many years of practice, it is still difficult for me at times, but I know there is no other way if you want a successful marriage. Much tension is caused by a refusal to take responsibility for our own actions. The first person who ever did this was Adam, when he said, 'The woman that thou gavest me.' (Gen. 3:12). He was really saying, 'It is her fault, not mine', with the insinuation, 'It is your fault God, you gave her to me.' We must take responsibility for our own actions.

The longer we hold out, the more tension grows. It is a lot easier to move a mole hill than it is to move a mountain.

Where love is really alive, there must be forgiveness constantly flowing. I have met some couples who have had problems over thirty years and not forgiven each other. I believe that to delay even an hour is too long! Asking for forgiveness takes the sting out of the situation and keeps love flowing. Husbands, wives, parents, children and in-laws need a lot of forgiving. The closer you are to people, the easier it is for them to hurt you!

It works!

We need to be known as forgiving people. Young people, get into the habit of forgiving now and maintain a spirit of forgiveness all the way through your life; then you will be truly blessed. Teach your children from the youngest age to ask forgiveness and to apologize. This is a vital part in the training and shaping of their lives. Then, when they are older and eventually marry and have a family of their own, they will be able to initiate forgiveness, because this attitude will be a natural, in-built part of their lives. If I know you are a forgiving person, I will have no fear of coming to you, because it means you love me and perfect love casts out all fear (1 John 4:18). But if I think you will be hard and callous towards me, I will never come to you and share anything. It is vital in our families that forgiveness is freely flowing. It is another key to keeping our relationships fresh.

Once I was sharing these things in a Saturday morning men's meeting in America. I concluded by saying, 'Every one of you go home, put your arms around your wife and tell her that you love her. Then ask her to forgive you for all the things that you have ever done wrong.'

That evening we had a big rally with hundreds of people present. At the end of the service, a very attractive and smartly dressed lady came up to me and looking me straight in the eyes, said, 'Mr Double, what did you do to my husband this morning?' I said, 'I do not know, you tell me'. To which she replied, 'He came home and put his arms around me and told me that he loved me! Do you know what he did next? He asked me to fogive him for all the things that he had ever done wrong, and he has never done that before, and it is wonderful!' That evening, although we had never met before, they took me out for a meal to celebrate!

10. The Great Divide

'Therefore a man shall leave his father and mother and be joined to his wife and they shall become one flesh.' (Genesis 2:24)

From the beginning, God planned that the marriage convenant made by two people should be a life-long, 'Till death us do part' relationship. Divorce was never God's intention. In fact, we are told that God hates divorce (Mal. 2:16). It is always the result of sin and causes hurt to those involved, especially the children.

However, divorce is so common these days that it must be faced. No longer is it just a problem encountered by movie stars, to which the rest of society is immune. Vast numbers of new converts are either divorced or divorced and remarried and are sincerely seeking to know where they stand as far as God's Word is concerned.

On one side our permissive society has offered the ultimate answer to divorce 'Don't get married, just live together'. The Church, however, has too often self-righteously retreated, relegating any divorcees and certainly any who are remarried to 'second class citizenship', treating them as social lepers. Some seem to consider divorce and remarriage as the 'unforgiveable sin'. Such casualties are instantly banned from preaching, holding a church office, counselling or even singing in the choir. This is usually done with no consideration as to the background, cause or biblical legitimacy of the divorce. Many Christians totally lack compassion in the area of divorce and adultery. Our attitiude should be the same as that of

Christ Jesus (Phil 2:5 NIV), which is clearly illustrated in the way He lovingly reacted towards the woman caught in the act of adultery. (John 8:3-11)

Many Christians assume that the Bible has nothing to say about divorce or simply condemns it. However, the Scriptures are certainly not silent concerning this area. So let us, laying aside our personal prejudices, come with an open heart to God's Word.

Although God hates divorce, he recognizes it and does not outrightly condemn it, but rather lays down clear principles concerning the matter.

In fact, God himself divorced Israel for her adultery! *'Then I saw that for all the causes for which backsliding Israel had committed adultery, I had put her away and given her a certificate of divorce'* (Jeremiah 3:8). Therefore, any who say, 'We will have nothing to do with anyone who is divorced', must include God in their excommunication! The Bible even records 113 divorces that took place to honour God (Ezra 10:12-19).

The Old Testament Law

> *'When a man takes a wife and marries her, and it happens that she finds no favour in his eyes because he has found some uncleanliness in her, and he writes her a certificate of divorce, puts it in her hand, and sends her out of his house, when she has departed from his house, and goes and becomes another man's wife, if the latter husband detests her and writes a certificate of divorce, puts it in her hand, and sends her out of his house, or if the latter husband dies who took her to be his wife, then her former husband who divorced her* must not *take her back to be his wife after she has been defiled; for that is an abomination before the Lord, and you shall not bring sin on the land which the Lord your God is giving you as an inheritance.'* (Deut. 24:1-4).

We see from this passage that under God's law an official bill of divorce can be signed and witnessed publicly, thus releasing a partner to remarry.

However, it had become an open practice (to avoid adultery) to divorce one's partner and to take another, on the grounds that if that new relationship did not work out, one could always go back to their original partner. God condemned these 'trial marriages'. He made it clear; if a person has remarried, then it is too late to change their mind! This realization should cause a person to seriously consider whether they wanted to *permanently* end their marriage, before marrying another. The divorce was final. Notice that the passage refers to 'former husband', not to her 'true husband'. The concept that two divorced people are 'still married in God's sight', as some have taught, is not only unscriptural but extremely harmful.

God hates divorce, but he does not outrightly condemn it. Not every divorce is sinful. Even if every divorce is the result of sin. Rather, the Lord lays down certain legitimate causes in His Word. Although divorce was introduced by men, due to their hardness of heart, in certain situations it is permitted by God. In 1 Corinthians Chapter 7, Paul considers the subject under two sections. Let us look at them together.

Section 1 – *The believer with an unbelieving partner.*

'If any brother has a wife who does not believe, and she is willing to live with him, let him not divorce her. And a woman who has a husband who does not believe, if he is willing to live with her, let her not divorce him. For the unbelieving husband is sanctified by the wife, and the unbelieving wife is sanctified by the husband; otherwise your children would be unclean, but now they are holy, But if the unbeliever departs, let him depart; a brother or sister is not under bondage in such cases. But God has called us to peace. For how do you know, O wife when you will save your husband? Or how do you know, O husband, whether you will save your wife.' (1 Cor. 7:12-16).

I often meet Christians who 'for an easy life', want to be separated from their unbelieving partner. Some even behave and talk in such a manner that heightens the problems and encourages a separation. This is clearly sin! Even if problems arise, any refusal to be reconciled must come from the unbeliever and never from the believer. The Christian is exhorted to do all that is possible to hold the marriage together, both for the unbeliever's sake (that they might come to know Christ by their exposure to the Gospel through their partner) and also for the children's sake. However, if the unbelieving partner demands a divorce, the believing partner is not to stand in the way for

> *'God has called us to peace.'* (1 Cor. 7:15)

Many believers hold on for years, refusing their partner a divorce, hoping for a reconciliation. However, this causes much tension, often driving the unbeliever to commit adultery.

I meet many Christian women, whose husbands have divorced them and re-married, who still say, 'I have a *word* that the Lord will bring him back and we will remarry.' However, as we have already seen, this clearly contradicts God's Word. (Deut. 24:1-4).

> *'If the unbeliever departs, let him depart; A brother or sister is not under bondage in such cases.'* (1 Cor. 7:15).

The word 'bound', 'doulos' in the Greek, means to 'enslave'. It was the word used of a slave who had an inseparable bond for life to his master. Yet if that bond was broken, the slave was from then onwards free of all ties and responsibility to his master. In other words, for such a person all the bonds and obligations of marriage have been removed. They are now a free person and released to remarry (only a Christian) if they wish.

Section 2 – *The believer with a believing partner.*

'To the married I command, yet not I but the Lord; a wife is not to depart from her husband. But even if she does depart, let her remain unmarried, or be reconciled to her husband. And a husband is not to divorce his wife.' (1 Cor. 7:10-11).

When two married believers are involved, they are commanded by God not to separate. Yet, even if they disobey God's command, they are not to remarry, thus leaving the door open for repentance and a re-establishment of their marriage. (Obviously to marry another would close the door to a reconciliation). God's Word gives only one legitimate ground for initiating divorce and remarriage and that is 'sexual immorality'.

'It has been said 'Whoever divorces his wife, let him give her a certificate of divorce' but I say to you that whoever divorces his wife for any reason except sexual immorality *causes her to commit adultery; and whoever marries a woman who is divorced commits adultery.'* (Mathew 5:31-32).
'Whoever divorces his wife, except for sexual immorality, *and marries another, commits adultery, and whoever marries her who is divorced commits adultery.'* (Mathew 19:9).

The authorized (King James) Version of the Bible translates the word 'sexual immorality' as 'fornication'. This has caused some confusion, as the word 'fornication', is today used to mean sexual sin by two unmarried people. However, the greek word, 'porneia' means far more than that. The word 'fornication' is used in cases of incest (1 Cor. 5:1), homosexuality (Jude 7) and even adultery (Jermiah 3:1,2,6,8,). The Greek word for adultery 'noichao' means 'unfaithfulness to a marriage partner', whereas Jesus chose a different word which includes 'unfaithfulness to a marriage partner' but means 'sexual sin of any kind'. Modern translations correctly translate the Greek word 'porneia' as 'sexual sin'. It includes homosexuality, lesbianism, bestiality and incest, as well as adultery. It was on the grounds of adultery that God divorced Israel. (Jeremiah 3:8 and Hosea 2:2).

It is important to see that, although sexual immorality can be grounds for divorce, such action is not necessary, nor is it inevitable. Rather, if the guilty party will repent, a reconciliation can take place, which is far better. God permitted divorce because of man's 'hardness of heart' (Mark 10:4 & 5). However, if a person will let God soften and change their heart, even if there has been sexual sin or unfaithfulness in the marriage, a reconciliation is possible.

Reconciliation should be sought wholeheartedly and divorce not even considered it there is any possibility of repentance and forgiveness. If there is a true repentance, the partner must forgive (Mathew 6:14-15) and obviously, divorce proceedings cannot continue after forgiveness has been granted. Although, according to the Jewish law an adulterer should be stoned to death, which would then release the other partner, Jesus gave the woman taken in the very act of adultery another chance (John 8:5). He did not condemn her, but told her to sin no more (verse 11).

Even after acts of unfaithfulness, a partner should always seek to forgive the other taking them back and giving another chance. Remarriage should *never* be considered until the door has been finally closed for reconciliation by the partner who has sinned remarrying. Under such circumstances, the Scriptures are clear that the person is then free to remarry.

Even then a person should follow the teaching of their local church and in no way take independent action to divorce and remarry without first consulting and getting the covering of their leadership. If your church teaches something contrary to what has been taught in this chapter, the commitment to that local church should be respected.

In spite of Isreal's sin, God called her back, making it clear that if she would repent and return, then he would forgive her and receive her back. He even took the initiative in seeking her out. Although, she had gone after other lovers the Lord said, 'I will allure her, will bring her into the wilderness, and speak comfort to her.' (Hosea 2:13-14). Even after Israel had 'played the prostitute' God said 'Return to me'. But 'she did not return.' 'When I saw that for all the causes for which backsliding Israel had committed adultery, I had put her away and given her a certificate of divorce' (Jeremiah 2:7-8).

The teaching that adultery automatically dissolves a marriage because 'a new one' has been set up is erroneous. Marriage authorizes sexual relationships, but they are not the same thing. If sex and marriage were the same, the guilty parties would have committed bigamy not adultery (Malachi 2:14).

Divorce, in cases of adultery, is the final course of action not the first! It is restricted to those cases where the unfaithful party refuses to repent of his or her sin and to be reconciled.

New Creatures

In today's society many people have already been divorced or remarried before becoming a Christian. I believe the Bible clearly teaches that God accepts us as we are and has put our past sin 'as far as the east is from the west' (Psalm 103:12), never to be remembered again! (Heb. 8:12, see also Heb. 10:17, Isa. 38:17, Jer. 31:34). We truly are a 'new creature', 'Old has passed away, behold *ALL* things have become new.' (2 Cor. 5:17). Therefore, God treats the new Christian as though they were single, and therefore free to remarry, as long as the door has been closed to a reconciliation with their previous partner.

It would be easy to jump straight into another marriage in the hope of finding healing from the past. However, this would be disastrous. Statistics show that the divorce rate for 'second time' marriages is higher than for 'first time' marriages. So often character faults that were involved in the first break up are not dealt with and can contribute to a second! An openness for God to deal with any such issues is vital if a future relationship is to work. There also needs to be a willingness for God to deal with any guilt, bitterness, resentment and past hurts. These are not areas to be skimmed over but will take time and may need working out with the help of another brother or sister. Only then should remarriage be considered.

11. Relating To Unsaved Members Of Our Families

'Now to the married I command, yet not I but the Lord; a wife is not to depart from her husband. But even is she does depart, let her remain unmarried or be reconciled to her husband and a husband is not to divorce his wife. But to the rest I, not the Lord, say; if any brother has a wife who does not believe, and she is willing to live with him, let him not divorce her, and a woman who has a husband who does not believe, if he is willing to live with her, let her not divorce him. For the unbelieving husband is sanctified by the wife and the unbelieving wife is sanctified by the husband; otherwise your children would be unclean, but now they are holy, But if the unbeliever departs, let him depart; a brother or a sister is not under bondage in such cases. But God has called us to peace. For how do you know, O wife, whether you will save your husband? Or how do you know, O husband, whether you will save your wife? (Corinthians 7:10-16)

Although there are not any techniques by which we can guarantee that our unsaved loved ones will be won for the Lord, the Maker's Instructions carry several very important principles which we need to adopt.

Stay in or come out?

The first principle set forth is, 'Let each one remain in the same calling to which he was called' (verse 20). In other words, when a person gets saved who is living with unsaved loved ones, they are to remain in that setting and not to run away from it. 'For how do you know, O wife, whether you will save your husband? Or how do you know, O husband, whether you will save your wife?' (verse 16) Our homes are the first place that we are called to evangelize. So, how do we relate to and reach our loved ones for the Lord?

1. Live a godly life. Many years back I used to sell to the meat department of a large store, what were called, 'shoulders of ham.' Really, it was third rate boiled bacon, but it was popular as it was half the price of real ham. It was edible, but anyone with discernment could tell the difference. If what we believe is not demonstrated by our lifestyle, our unsaved loved ones will soon see the difference and we will never win them. My mother and father were angry when I first got saved, especially when I was baptized in water. They told me in no uncertain terms that I had made a fool of them and let them down. Since then, to the glory of God, they have both been converted and filled with the Holy Spirit. Today they are two of my biggest fans, but they tested me! Our loved ones need to know that the Lord means all to us, and that we are prepared for them to test the reality of Christ in our lives.

We are told to have our conduct 'honourable among the gentiles, that when they speak against you as evildoers, they may, by your good works which they *observe*, glorify God in the day of visitation' (1 Peter 2:12). Our lifestyle is to be honourable among those who are unsaved, for if we sow righteous works, there is a day coming when they are going to glorify God for what they have seen. The principle of sowing and reaping is clearly seen here, 'What a man sows, that will he also reap.' Therefore, be encouraged if you have been sowing for a while and yet there seems to have not been much reaping. The Scriptures promise that if we 'cast our bread upon the waters', it shall return to us after many days. God is going to make sure that somewhere along the line there is a day of visitation, where His presence will become so real that our loved ones cannot deny it. Then they are going to glorify God for the righteous things which we have done. The Scriptures go on to say, 'Likewise you wives, be submissive to your husbands, that even if they do not obey the word, they, *without a word*, may be won by the *conduct* of their wives, when they *observe* your chaste conduct accompanied by fear.' (1 Peter 3:1-2). It is not necessarily the spoken word that is going to win a person, but our conduct and lifestyle; the Word made flesh, the way in which we live. Actions speak louder than words! Although this Scripture refers to the wife, it is a sound principle for any member of the family. If our actions do not match up to our words, anything we seek to share is nullified and often the one we are seeking to reach is hardened even more against the Gospel.

Notice the passage's reference to our 'chaste conduct, accompanied by fear.' That fear is the fear of the Lord. Do our unsaved loved ones recognize the fear of God in our lives? We will never win them by compromising. They know what reality is and soon recognize unreality. God can never work through compromise. If you sin in front of the unsaved members of your family, do not try to cover it up or make excuses. Open your heart up and admit you were wrong. Then apologize and ask their forgiveness.

2. *Love the Lord wholeheartedly*. Jesus said, 'Do not think that I come to bring peace on the earth, I did not come to bring peace but a sword. For I have come to set a man against his father, a daughter against a mother, and a daughter-in-law against her mother-in-law. A man's foes will be those of his own household. He who loves father or mother more than me is not worthy of me. And he who loves son or daughter more than me is not worthy of me. And he who does not take his cross and follow after me is not worthy of me. He who finds his life will lose it and he who loses his life for my sake will find it' (Mathew 10:34-39).

If you love another more than you love Christ, then you

are going to be in trouble. However, the more you love Christ the more you will love those close to you. Therefore, a way of increasing your love for them is by making sure that Jesus has His rightful place in your life.

Jesus told a parable about a man that gave a party, various people were invited and they responded by making a variety of excuses. One answer came back, 'I have married a wife and therefore I cannot come' (Luke 14:20). It sounds quite reasonable, but Jesus did not have mercy on that person, but spoke quite strongly against them. Whether it is a husband, a wife, a parent or a child, we have no excuse for saying that we cannot go Christ's way. Jesus said, 'I say to you that none of those men who were invited shall taste my supper' (Luke 14:24). A common statement is, 'I cannot meet together with Christ's people because my partner does not like it.' We need to genuinely and honestly search our hearts as to whether this is true. I have found it rare that a husband will not release his wife to at least one meeting a week. A downright refusal is usually the result of insensitivity in the past and a neglecting of the family for church activities.

Baby-sitting is sometimes used as an excuse for missing gathering together with God's people. Although this can be a very genuine reason, one should not hide behind the fact that they have a baby. Their heart attitude should be, 'I desire to be gathered with God's people, but my responsibility to my child, means that for the present I cannot.'

Jesus also said, 'If anyone comes to me and does not hate his father and mother, wife and children, brothers and sisters, yes, and his own life also, he cannot be my disciple. And whoever does not bear his cross and come after me he cannot be my disciple.' (Luke 14:26)

Here again we see the great principle of loving Christ above everything else. Our love for Christ should be so great, that it makes our love for others look like hate.

Our youngest child, Faith, was born about two weeks late. I had planned a ministry trip to Japan so that Faith would be born, and Heather settled back at home before I set off. With Faith turning up late, it left me with a real crisis in my own heart. It was Heather, with Faith only two hours old, who said, 'You are not cancelling your ministry trip to Japan, God wants you there. He will take care of me. You go.' So I went, with both Heather and I knowing it was right and what God wanted. Soon after I arrived back we were at a Convention where a woman came up to me and said, 'I have got something against you Mr. Double and I have to get it sorted out.' I asked what it was and she replied, 'You left your wife two or three days after she had a baby and went off to Japan. That is not right.' I explained to her the cost that was involved and how Heather had encouraged me to go. To this woman, my actions looked like hatred of my wife, but what she never saw was our love for the Lord that caused it to happen. This love must be above everything else. This will certainly give us a better relationship with God, a greater peace in our own heart and more love for our relatives.

3. Do not compromise. The fact that there is a division on Kingdom principles has to be faced. Every time your life changes, it is going to be a challenge to others. In Strangeways prison earlier this year, I met a man who had recently been converted. That very weekend he had received a reply from his wife, after writing to tell her that he had become a Christian. He had told her how it had changed his life and that he was looking forward to being with her again. She had written back saying, 'I do not want you to change. I like you as a criminal and want you to stay that way.' There have been occasions where people have literally had to leave, 'For the Gospel's sake'. In Eastern Europe, for example, loved ones are constantly being separated for 'the Gospel's sake'. If you live in a spiritualist's house or the home of someone who practices black magic you may well be forced to get out and leave that loved one for 'the Gospel's sake'.

If you live in a very immoral home, you may have to

leave. The Scriptures make it clear, Christ must come first. However, I must stress that what I have just related is very unusual, but it does from time to time happen. I have known occasions, where for various reasons it would have been wrong for the person to continue to live in a certain situation, where they would be party to extreme sin. Jesus said, 'Everyone who has left houses or brothers or sisters or father or mother or wife or children or lands, *for my Name's sake*, shall receive a hundredfold, and inherit everlasting life' (Mathew 19:29).

'Assuredly I say to you, there is no one who has left house or parents or brothers or wife or children, *for the sake of the Kingdom of God*, who shall not receive many times more in this present time and in the age to come eternal life' (Luke 18:29-30).

We see very clearly here that there is no other reason for leaving our loved ones, than for 'Christ's' or the 'Kingdom's' sake. I would add here, when I say leave, I am not talking necessarily about a parting in the sense of ceasing to live with them, but *a dividing of the ways as far as our actions are concerned*. However, if it ever came to a permanent thing, God gives us a promise that we are going to receive one hundred fold! We cannot lose out by going God's way. The way of compromise always loses!

4. Love your relatives. They need love beyond something emotional or sentimental. Doing is love in action. Seek to be the *best* wife, husband, son, daughter or parent in the world. This involves caring and having an interest in them as a person. So often, sadly, when a member of the family is converted, because their interests are no longer the same they lose interest in unsaved relatives too. This will drive them away instead of winning them. Obviously there has got to be a line on this and you must not be involved in anything unrighteous. But, you can pay an interest in righteous things. I doubt if anyone reading this book has a loved one who only has unrighteous interests.

There is a big difference between being righteous and being religious! Jesus was righteous, but He was not religious.

Notice, that it was always the religious He offended, not the world. He seemed at home with tax collectors, prostitutes and sinners, though He himself remained sinless. Instead of avoiding Him, the unsaved wanted Him around. He was not threatened by them, but neither did they feel 'got at' by Him. Rather, there was something attractive and winning about Him. Levi, the tax collector, even put on a great feast in his own home for Jesus. But, 'When the scribes and Pharisees saw him eating with the tax collectors and sinners, they said to his disciples, 'How is it that he eats and drinks with tax collectors and sinners?' When Jesus heard it, he said to them, 'Those who are well have no need of a physician, but those who are sick. I did not come to call the righteous, but sinners to repentance' (Mark 2:16).

Jesus said, 'To whom then shall I liken the men of this generation and what are they like? They are like children sitting in the market-place and calling one another, saying: "We played the flute for you, And you did not dance; We mourned to you, And you did not weep;" For John the Baptist came neither eating bread nor drinking wine, and you say "He has a demon." The Son of the Man has come eating and drinking, and you say, "Look, a glutton and a wine bibber, a friend of tax collectors and sinners!" (Luke 7:31-34)

So often Christians are seen to be boring. Jesus came that we might have life, and 'have it more abundantly' (John 10:10). He came that we might enjoy life to the full. So many Christians act unnaturally when in the presence of unbelievers, rather than relaxing and letting the life of God shine through.

Seek to be the best friend your loved one has. Accept them as they are at this moment. That is how Christ accepted you. So often believers expect Christian behaviour from their non-Christian relatives. This is an unfair expectation. We need to remember that anything good in our lives is the result of God's working! Rather than complain, we should be grateful for any good points they may have! We must accept them as they are, for love has an amazing transforming effect.

5. *Do not preach at them.* This is one way of driving your relatives away. I heard of one wife who tried to win her husband by pea-shooting Gospel texts at him every time he came home. The poor man would be sitting eating a meal and she would preach at him from the other side of the room. Even when he went to bed at night, there was a tract under his pillow!

Do not try to nag them into the Kingdom! You will never win anyone in this way. Arguing is not the way either. I am regularly asked by wives with unsaved husbands how to bring them to the Lord. I often tell them, 'Stop preaching at him. Stop arranging for other Christians to come in *just* to have a word with him. Start seeking to be the best wife in the world to him. Start complimenting him. Cook his favourite meals for him. Make sure that his socks are darned and his buttons are in place. Sit on his knee. Love him. Make sure that you satisfy him sexually. Then it will not be long before he says, 'What has happened to you?' Then you can say, 'The Lord Jesus has just put such a love in my heart for you. Wouldn't you like to get to know Him too?'

6. *Seek to persuade them.* Although we are not to preach to our unsaved relations, the Bible does encourage us to seek to persuade them (2 Corinthians 5:11). Believe for those moments when you can gently open up and share something about the Lord. Ask God to give you a sensitivity to your loved ones. From time to time invite them to special meetings and events. However, be gentle, considerate and sensitive in how you do it. I remember a time when we use to regularly have Church parties, with a little epilogue at the end. Any time someone had a birthday or anniversary in the Church, we would have an outreach party and the Church would invite others in. These were great friendly evenings together, with sticky buns, coffee and cakes and no end were won to the Lord that way. Often, relaxed funtimes break down many of the barriers unsaved loved

ones have and kill many 'religious' concepts of Christianity.

Encourage friends from the Church to informally come to your home; this way they can meet your unsaved family on their own territory. Many Christians are shy about doing this. However, I believe it should be the most natural thing. Do not go inviting 'Hot Gospellers', they will only put your family off, but inviting Christian friends in for a cup of tea or for a meal can be very effective. Often this will lead to further opportunities to do things together, like playing squash or football, going swimming or sharing in other areas of similar interests. Even if they make mistakes or 'put their foot in it', they are not going to do the harm you may think they will. Ensure that you do not behave unnaturally because there are other Christians around, nor sit and talk continually about Christian things, leaving the unsaved one feeling left out of things.

Often as I travel around, I am placed in homes where there is an unsaved partner. This is often done deliberately, with people thinking, 'He's an evangelist. He'll win them to the Lord.' I have won a few to the Lord, but I did not use the tactics they expected of me. If I stay in a home where there is an unsaved person. One of my goals is to talk to them more than I talk to the saved people. I try to find a level at which we can relate. This is the kind of person you want to bring into your home to share with your relatives.

I remember on one occasion being shown into a businessman's home. His wife was a Christian, but he was not. After much prayer on their behalf, he had condescended to letting me stay there. After being introduced, we began to chat over a cup of coffee, talking about his business and other interests in his life. Soon the conversation got around to the subject of football, so I asked him, 'Do you watch 'Match of the Day?' He replied, 'Yes, I like 'Match of the Day', do you?' I said, 'Yes, can we watch it together tonight?' He agreed and so when I returned from the meeting that evening, he already had the television on. I took off my shoes, put my feet up and made myself at home. We became quite friendly and the next day he came to the Sunday night meeting and was saved! Building on a righteous basis, requires an interest in the person. Not once did that man feel got at by me.

7. *Pray for them.* Even before my children and grandchildren were born, I began to pray for them to be saved. We need to get before the Lord and seek Him for a burden for each member of our family. 'The earnest heartfelt, continued prayer of a righteous man makes tremendous power available dynamic in its working' (James 5:16 Amplified Bible).

This is what is required for your loved one. Don't give up. Believe that out of your praying, dynamic power is going to be made available. If they are going to be converted to Christ, it will only be real when the dynamic power of God has been involved. You could go on hoping or praying in unbelief forever. The real requirement is heartfelt continued prayer! If you love someone your praying will be heartfelt. So much prayer for unsaved relatives is motivated by selfishness rather than a love for them and awareness that without Christ they are destined for an eternity in separation from God. So much prayer for the unsaved is motivated by the attitude, 'It would be so lovely and much easier for me if my partner were saved.' Primarily, do we desire them to be saved for their benefit or ours? We need Christ to change our hearts so that our prayers are rightly motivated and really heartfelt. Also if we love someone, our prayers will be continued, we won't give up! It is this heartfelt continued prayer which brings God's power into the situation. Often our timing is different to God's. Do not get discouraged or give up praying, but rather, continue to stay in faith for them. Study God's Word and discover his promises concerning the family. Typical examples are:

> *'I will establish my covenant with you and your descendants after you.'* (Genesis 9:9).

'I will pour my Spirit on your descendants, And my blessing on your offspring . . .One will say, 'I am the Lord's; . . . . Another will write with his hands 'The Lord's . . .' (Isaiah 44:3)

'Believe in the Lord Jesus Christ, and you will be saved, you and your household.' (Acts 16:31) (See also Deuteronomy 30:19, Acts 3:25)

There is no substitute for God's Word in producing faith in your heart. If you merely pray out of sentiment, you will soon get frustrated and give up. It is God's Word that brings us the strength to hold on in faith, even if there seems to be no evidence of change. We are probably more able to pray for them effectively than anyone else, because we are so close to them. If we are sensitive to the Lord He can show us how to pray about the details of their lives and how He can really effect them.

Finally, we all need a very precious fruit of the Spirit called patience. Do not become impatient. Pray that God will give you patience. Settle that God wants your unsaved family in His kingdom more than you do and that by living righteously, all out for the Lord, taking any opportunities He gives, loving and showing an interest in them, you will reach them for Christ.

12. Parents And Children

'And you fathers, do not provoke your children to wrath, but bring them up in the training and admonition of the Lord'

(Ephesians 6:4.)

In these days, it is important that our children are brought up according to the 'Maker's Instructions' otherwise they do not stand a chance in life.

Note firstly, that fathers are told not to *provoke* their children to wrath. The way to avoid doing this, is to encourage and 'provoke them to love and good works' (Heb. 10:24). It is so important to encourage your children and to believe the very best for them. I encourage my children to be the best at school and aim to be around the top of the class in everything.

Never, never (a million times never) tell your children that they are failures or hopeless. This can cause deep-seated scars which come out years later, as we frequently find when counselling adults. Tell you children that, with God's help, they are going to make an impact in life and believe for the very best for them all the way through.

One way in which to provoke our children to anger is by being unreasonable. Some parents, who have forbidden their children to do a certain thing, when asked by the child 'Why?', give the reply 'Because I said so'. This is provoking your child to anger! When we do have to say 'no', we should take time to teach our children the reason for our decisions. You will gain your children's respect by doing this.

Discipline

In many schools today, discipline is almost non-existent and contrary to God's word. As a result, our children often find their school companions doing the opposite to what we are teaching. This causes them to ask questions and we need to be able to explain to them why our attitudes and standards are different. We need to take time to teach them the principles of God's Word. For many people, discipline is a knotty problem, but it is one of the most challenging things in today's society. We have a golden opportunity to present the Gospel by disciplining our children, the world will notice the difference in them and have to admit that it works. One of the reasons society today is being destroyed is the failure of parents to discipline their children. Much of the rioting on our streets is the result of young people growing up without discipline. Some psychiatrists and psychologists have told us that if we spank and discipline our children we are going to make them violent. This is totally unscriptural and leads to the violence we now see amongst both children and adults. Delinquent children are often the result of delinquent parents, who have failed to discipline and train them properly. If you want to know what you are like, look at your children.

A home without discipline will be a chaotic home. Stephen, when he was 16 years old, said at one of our family services, 'I am glad that both my parents discipline me. I have seen boys at school who go around boasting that their parents do not discipline them and I have seen the mess that their lives are in.'

I stay in so many Christian homes where the children are boss because they know just how to manipulate their parents. To me this is a disgrace. Parents need to have authority in the home.

The Bible says: 'He who spares his rod *hates* his son. But he who loves him disciplines him promptly' (Prov. 13:24). You may say that by not using the rod, you are loving your child, but God calls it hate. When they become adults, you will see the result but then it will be too late. Why do we have to use the rod? Our hand should be a representation of love to our children. On occasions I have had to use my hand on my children because there was no rod available, but if it is a regular symbol of correction to your child, it will cause confusion. That is the reason God says use a rod. 'Foolishness is bound up in the heart of a child, but the rod of correction will drive it far from him' (Prov. 22:15). Many children's hearts are full of foolishness because they have not been punished as the Bible says. We need to ensure that we discipline according to the 'Maker's Instructions'.

'Chasten thy son while there is hope, and let not thy soul spare for his crying' (Prov. 19:18). A father and mother need to be strong and not moved by the tears of their children. Tears can be a manipulating force, so you must not allow them to influence you. 'Do not withold correction from a child: if you beat him with a rod, he will not die' (Prov. 23:13). Discipline is not only a physical thing, but it is a spiritual thing also. 'He will not die spiritually.' If a child grows up constantly getting his own way with his parents, he will always want his own way with God too.

Proverbs 23:14 tells us, 'You shall beat him with a rod, and deliver his soul from hell.' When you teach your child obedience, you are teaching him to obey God. I have five children, two of them are in full-time service today, who have gone through the so-called 'difficult teenage stage'. Although I do not want to pretend that they did not have any problems, they have come through victorious and have never been completely away from God, because they were taught and disciplined all the way through. I am believing too for Stephen and Joel, who are in their teenage years, that they will also come through victoriously. 'The rod and reproof give wisdom, but a child left to himself brings shame to his mother' (Prov. 29:15).

In today's society, child abuse has sadly become rampant. This is often the result of parents losing self-control. The reason is that so often discipline is the final result and made out of anger. Discipline should be administered calmly, with a clear reason for the punishment, followed by love and forgiveness. The subject should then be forgotten and not brought up again. Sending or taking your child to another room will give time for any anger in you to abate. Never correct out of anger but seek to manifest love. Correction, according to 'the Maker's Instructions' is a true hallmakr of love for 'Whom the Lord loves He chastens and scourges every child He receives' (Heb. 12:5,6).

It hurts me more than it hurts my children when I have to discipline them but soon we are cuddling and making up. I find that my children love me more after discipline than they did before.

God's way works

'When the wicked are multiplied, transgression increases: but the righteous will see their fall. Correct your son, and he will give you rest: yes, he will give you delight to your soul', (Prov. 29:16,17). The child that is disciplined delights his parents' soul.

Some parents threaten their children with the words 'If you do that again I will smack you'; yet fail to carry out the punishment. This is teaching them to lie. They will never believe what you or anyone else says, including God. You must always carry out a threat – whatever the cost. Children will often push to see how far they can go and at what point you will keep your word. The longer you continue to threaten your child, but put off keeping your word, the less respect you will have and the harder it will be to keep discipline.

A lack of instant discipline will result in a nervous child. Mothers must therefore be prepared to discipline their children instantly, not threatening the child to 'wait until daddy comes home.' This will make the child nervous, wondering what punishment awaits them. It will also create a wrong relationship between them and their father, based on fear.

Another common practice amongst parents is 'bribing' children to do things. Such statements as, 'Mummy will give you an ice cream if you do the job,' are neither good for them, nor do they build a godly serving attitude. They need to learn to respond out of obedience to their parents, without any ulterior motives.

It is vital that a mother and father never disagree over discipline in front of their children. This probably causes more harm than anything else a parent ever does. It helps to teach the child, among other things, how to manipulate and play one parent off against the other. I believe that every home needs clearly defined boundary lines, and that correction should be given whenever these lines are crossed.

The only time discipline ceases, is when they get married and leave home. A child is called to obey his parents until then. There is no teaching in the Bible about eighteen or twenty-one or any other age being a time when a child ceases to be under discipline. While they are in your house, they are under your authority and therefore under your discipline.

Of course, you have to be wise when they get older, so that you do not treat them as five year olds. As a child matures, so you can give him greater freedom, but still clear boundaries are required.

Our son Nigel, who today is a Church leader, as a teenager had to be in at night by 10.00 p.m. When he was sixteen he had a motorcycle. We could tell the time by hearing his motorcycle come up the road most evenings at 9.59 p.m. He would never be late unless there was a good reason, when he would telephone to say what had happened. He knew what the punishment for disobedience of this boundary would be. There are times that

I will give an extension to this boundary, but only after sitting down with them to find out exactly what they are going to be doing, where they will be and the exact time we can expect them home. It is harmful to children to be allowed to come in at whatever time they like, even the early hours of the morning.

'For this reason a man shall leave his father and mother and be joined to his wife, and the two shall become one flesh' (Eph. 5:31). It is at marriage that our children cease to come under our control. When your children are married, let them go. On the eve of our children's wedding day, we tell them, 'From tomorrow on, you are free from our authority. You are under God's covering. We will never interfere in your life and your marriage. We will never poke our noses into your affairs. But we want you to know that if you ever need help, we are here. You can come any time. We will give you all the help we can, but we will only give it when it is asked for'.

Those teenage years

Often when children enter their teenage years, they go through a time when they want to experience things for themselves. Until then, even if their relationship with the Lord has been very real, it has probably been greatly influenced by their parents. There comes a time when any second hand experience in not enough, they have got to prove God for themselves. This may manifest itself in a little bit of flirting with the world and sometimes a deep flirting. It is at this time that parents need to be very prayerful and sensitive to God. They also need great care in the handling of their children. It is important that they do not despair, but stay in faith and walk with God through it all.

One of my children, for instance, was having quite a rough time in this area. God spoke to me and said that I should sacrifice everything else and give my spare time at home to my son. The big thing that was really needed was friendship from Dad. I avoided preaching at him or talking about my faith all the time. We just enjoyed life together. We went ten pin bowling, out for meals, played billiards and visited people together. I took an interest in the music he enjoyed, rather than condemning it without knowing what it was about. We listened to it together, and although I spoke out strongly against anything I thought was evil, some of it, I learned to enjoy myself. He began learning to drive on his seventeenth birthday, so Heather and I spent quite a lot of time taking him out in the car.

This worked successfully and over a short period of time, brought about a remarkable change. It was what God had said to me and obedience to Him brought victory.

It is so vital that parents are friends with their children. Prior to my conversion, I was quite a football fan, in reality my love of sport was probably touching on idolatry, which I had repented of. So for at least 12 years I did not go near a football match. One Boxing Day morning I was having a shave when God spoke to me with absolute clarity and said, 'I want you to take Nigel to the football today.' You could have blown me down with shock, but it was certainly the voice of God. I obeyed and it really did something for Nigel and I in our relationship.

Training

Train up a child in the way he should go, and when he is old he will not depart from it' (Prov. 22:6). This is a command with a promise. If you train your child right, God's Word says that he will not depart from it.

This is not only training them in spiritual things. We need to train them how to be obedient citizens in society and how to behave at school, respecting their school teachers and those in authority over them. We need to train them how to be good workers, so that when they find employment they are not going to strike, but work as unto the Lord, 'not with eye-service as men pleasers,' but being the very best for God in all that they do (Eph. 6:7).

God has made you stewards of your children. Therefore, seek to discover and develop the qualities and gifts that He has put within them. Do not try to make them clones of a brother or a sister, for God has made each child unique, so teach and train them to be themselves. Do not try to make them something you wanted to be as a child, but never became.

Decisions, Decisions, Decisions

Teach your children how to make the right decisions. If you make all the decisions for them, they will never learn how to discern right from wrong. Sometimes my children will come to me and say, 'Dad, can I do this?' I often say, 'Go away and ask the Lord, then come back and tell me what He says.' I do not give my authority away. I always retain the authority to override their decision. However, I would not do that unless I really had to, as I want my children to learn that I trust them.

T.V. Times

The television is a real arch-enemy of training children. Parents often use their T.V. as a baby sitter. They stick their child in front of the T.V. set for long periods of time to let them occupy themselves. I believe that this is both dangerous and unhealthy. Television is used to shape children's lives more than the lifestyle of their parents. What a child receives into their mind in those early formative years is very, very important. Some of the violence, filth and occult practices, that come over, even in children's programmes are so unhealthy for our children. I believe that parents should be very strict in censoring the programmes and wherever possible should view them with their children. If something is wrong that the child has looked at, the parents should us it as an aid to teach them how to make right choices.

We need to train them how to be a good husband or

wife. Teach your son how to handle his finances, how not to become tangled up in the hire purchase credit card craze, but to live within his means. Many marriages break down within months or even weeks, because the husband signs all kinds of HP commitments. Then at the end of the first month he receives all the bills, which he cannot pay. Teach them how to shop around and be good stewards of what they have. Train them how to do practical jobs around the home like being good gardeners. This will stand them in good stead for married life as home grown vegetables can take pressure off the housekeeping and the family's income. The garden can also be a lovely environment for family fun and a source of beautiful flowers to present to their wives.

Teach your daughters how to be good cooks, how to sew, knit and mend, make and take care of their clothes. Teach them how to clean and care for the home; how to cultivate a serving attitude that is willing to sacrifice personal preferences to serve the family. They will thank you for it later on, even if they moan now.

I was once staying in the home of a Christian family where the teenage girl had her fiancé staying for the weekend. She wanted to cook him breakfast so she asked him what he would like. He said that he would like a boiled egg. So she got the saucepan and put the egg in. One and a half hours later, she went to her father and asked him if he thought the egg was ready yet! This is not a far-fetched story, but the truth. I looked at the girl and thought, 'Poor lass, her mother has failed her.'

Responsibilities around the home, like emptying the rubbish bin, setting the table, washing or drying up, hoovering certain rooms, cleaning the car, watering the greenhouse, keeping the garage tidy etc., bring a sense of belonging. They also build godly principles into your children. Teach them, not just by words, but by doing the jobs with them. It would be easy with young children, to get frustrated and say, 'I could do it quicker myself.' However, this would be of no help to them. Encouraging them to do things is an important part of training, even if it means putting things right after they have finished! No child is too young to start having an input into the family. After they have done a job, seek to encourage them.

Teach your children to be positive and not to allow negative thoughts to fill their minds. This will prevent them becoming chronic depressives later on in life. Fill them with the positive teaching of God's Word. 'I can't' is usually an excuse for laziness.

Teach them how to give, and to realize that society does not owe them a living. We should teach our children to give from the very beginning so that they grow up to be generous people.

Our children tithed from the day they were born. When people give them gifts of money, after a few weeks we add it up and pay their tithe into the church. As they grow in understanding, we teach them to do it themselves. They never know what it is not to tithe. They never know what it is not to give. They are taught from the beginning to be generous.

Teach your children how to love. Do not be afraid to express love openly to one another in front of the child. For example, it is good to kiss your wife in front of the children and let them see that you love each other. If you teach your children what love is and how to love, they are far less likely to relate to the opposite sex wrongly and after marrying someone, find out that it was only lust. Lust never lasts, love always lasts.

I'm not your Mum!

There are a lot of homes where you hear the husband calling the wife, 'Mum.' You may say he is doing it for the children's sake, but it is not right. It creates a wrong image and there may be more implications behind it. Often there is something in that person's life causing them to call their spouse, 'Mother ,' or 'Father.' Heather and I have a blitz on this if we hear it in the home and correct each other. We hear so many people doing it that it can just slip out. We come to grips with it because we believe it is very wrong. Some may feel that this is petty, but I see it as very important. The man that God has given you is your husband. Treat him as such. The woman that God has given you is your wife. Treat her as such. You are husband and wife and no other type of relationship should come in to spoil it.

We must see our partner as God intended them to be. Take as an example the case of a wife who has not had a good relationship with her father. Perhaps he left home, or he died, or he was there but just as a figure head. So when she got married she begins to see her partner, not only as her husband, but also as a father and drew from him what she would have had from her father. In the same way some men look upon their wives as a mother figure.

Honour when honour is due

It is important that our children learn that life is not 'fair'. In the story of the Prodigal Son, we see two basic wrong attitudes (Luke 15:11-32). One son 'used' his father; this was the more obvious sin of the two. Also the elder brother became jealous, feeling his father had treated him unfairly. Another example is the jealous reaction of Joseph's brothers at their father's gift to his son. Our children must learn to enjoy other people being honoured, especially family members. Taking time to teach these principles to our children will bring joy to us and them. Some parents, when one child has a birthday, insist on buying gifts for all the children. This does not teach them to honour others. 'If one members suffers all the members suffer with it; or if one member is honoured all the members rejoice with it' (1 Cor. 12:26). I am not teaching favouritism, which of course is wrong and very harmful. Each of my children are my favourites!

Sorry

One other principle which we need to ensure is built into our children's lives is the ability to say sorry. An hour spent patiently waiting for one of our children to come to the place of being able to say sorry, resulted in an adult who can now freely forgive and be forgiven. Time spent in training our children should never be seen as wasted time, but an investment in a life valuable to God. The best way to teach principles to a child is to demonstrate them as parents. Your being able to say sorry to your child when you are wrong, will be the quickest way to teach them. There have been times when we as parents have spoken wrongly, had a wrong attitude or passed the wrong judgement and have had to go to one of our children and say sorry and ask forgiveness. It has been so encouraging, for we have seen them respect us more as a result of such actions. Never have we sensed that we have gone down in their estimation.

All things new

I am often asked by parents, to whom God has spoken concerning their failure in disciplining their children in the past or where the husband has failed to lead the family, how to communicate their change of heart to the children and how to avoid just becoming disciplinarians, as discipline in these areas which I have shared about, must come out of a relationship. Firstly, there needs to be a family meeting where the parents can honestly apologize and ask their children's forgiveness for failing to shape their lives thus far. If teenagers are involved this still needs to be done, sharing what the approach will be in the future. It might be helpful to give them a week to adjust before the scriptural methods of discipline are applied. There may be some 'reactions' to start with, but you will need to deal with them by being committed to God's Word and He will honour it.

If you wish to be good parents, remember we were not born that way. We become good parents by seeking God and desiring to be the best parents possible to our children, always bearing in mind that we ourselves are still being taught by Him.

What we do as parents will affect our whole family, Because of Achan's sin, his whole family was destroyed. Because of Abraham's obedience, his whole family were blessed!

How to raise delinquent children

First — *Begin in infancy* by giving the child *everything he wants*. This is the way to make him grow up to believe the world owes him a living.

Second — When he picks up bad words, *laugh at him*. This will make him think he is cute.

Third — *Never* give him religious *training*. Wait till he is *twenty-one* and then let him decide for himself.

Fourth — Never say, *'That's wrong!'* It may develop a guilt complex or condition him to believe, when he is arrested for stealing, that society is against him and he is being persecuted.

Fifth — *Pick up everything he leaves lying around. Do everything for him*. He will then be experienced in throwing *all responsibility on to others*.

Sixth — *Let him read* anything he can get his hands on. Keep the house clean, but let his mind feast on garbage.

Seventh — Quarrel frequently in the *presence* of your children. Then they won't be too *shocked* when the home breaks up later.

Eight — Give the child *all* the pocket money he wants. Why should things be as tough for him as they were for you?

Ninth — Give him everything he wants to eat and

drink. Surfeit him with sweets. Denial may lead to harmful frustration.

Tenth Always *take his side against neighbours*, teachers and policeman. They are all prejudiced against your child.

Eleventh When he gets into real trouble, *excuse* yourself by saying, 'We never could do anything with him.'

Twelth *Prepare for a life of grief. You're likely to have it.*

(A Canadian Police Pamphlet)

13. Fatherhood

When a person is born again, God should cease to be just God to them. It is not that He has changed, as the only one deserving our worship, devotion and commitment. He is still God, but at the same time He wants to enter into a father/child relationship with us. He has 'sent forth the Spirit of His Son into your hearts crying Abba Father!' (Galatians 14:6) Many Christians have problems in relating to God as Father because they have never known what a real father is like. As one person put it, 'Talking to me about a father is like speaking to me in a foreign language.' This is hardly surprising with the rocketing divorce rate and a general breakdown in family life. Many of today's young people have never known a real father/child relationship and the word 'father' only stirs memories of pain and hurt, instead of the feeling of comfort and assurance which it should bring.

Our understanding of fatherhood must come from God, not from the world. The media in particular gives a false picture of father figures, that adversely affects family life. For instance, next time you see a television programme (especially a comedy), with a father in the cast, notice carefully he is portrayed. You will almost certainly find the image presented at variance with what God's Word teaches. Yet that same Word is the only reliable source of information we have on fatherhood. Our supreme example is God, 'the Father of us all'. The best way for a child to learn about fatherhood is from a father who models the character of God.

Everyone needs a father figure in their lives, not just children and there is a lack of 'fathers in God' today.

Many people are echoing in their hearts the words of Philip, 'Lord show us the Father.' (John 14:8) I believe that fatherhood on earth is important to people being able to relate in reality to God as their Father. Paul said to both individuals and whole churches that they were to take him as a 'model'. He also told the Christians at Corinth, 'For though you might have ten thousand instructors in Christ, yet you do not have many fathers, for in Christ Jesus I have begotten you through the Gospel.' (1 Corinthians 4:15) Fatherhood includes providing love, security, leadership, affection, acceptance, and comfort. Everyone needs to experience the love of a human father. People often come up to me and say, 'Mr Double, will you give me a father hug, I have never had one before.' That includes boys and girls, teenagers, and even adults!

Fatherly love

The Pasalmist described God's love as 'better than life.' How precious love is. In fact, you can only trust someone who loves you. The Bible tells us that, 'There is not fear in love but perfect love casts out fear, because fear involves torment.' (1 John 4:18) There should be no fear in a father/child relationship. Every child needs to know that they can come and talk *anything* through with their father without being afraid.

Children need to know that dad's ear is always available and that even though his answer may be 'no', he will listen and justly consider what they say. Many fathers are so austere, hard, religious, or just too busy to sit and listen. As a consequence many young people get their lives in a mess because they were afraid to sit and talk the issue through with their parents when the problems first began. Children need a father; someone who belongs to them; someone who wants them because they are his. Being a father is far more than a title, given to a certain member of the family. Relationship is at the core.

Fatherhood is far more than just being a 'guardian'.

That can be just a legal function, often lacking in real relationship. Sometimes there is a real relationship between the mother and the child but infrequently with the father. One couple even told me that they fostered for a living, as a job! God wants in a new way to 'Turn the hearts of the fathers to their children and the hearts of the children to their fathers' (Malachi 4:16).

Fatherly security

A long while ago now, two Americans sang a song in one of our meetings, the words of which really struck me,

'He loves you when you're right, and He loves you when you're wrong.'

That is how God is. It is also how we should be with each other. I would love my children, whatever I discovered about them. My love for them is never on the line! In fact, the more I find a person has failed or sinned deeply, somehow I feel that they need my love more.

Every child needs to know that there is a place in the family that belongs to them. A place which is their size, has their name on it, a place which nobody else can take away!

I think back to my dear father. However much trouble I got in, Dad was always there. I thank God for that. I never have had a problem relating to God as Father, because of my father's example. He is a poor man today, because of the things I did as a teenager. Now he is an old man, I feel that I owe it to him to care for him.

After children leave home, they still have a responsibility to honour their parents.

It is so sad the way that the old people are often treated. Many children opt out of their responsibility putting their parents in old people's homes. There are a lot of broken-hearted people in such places. George Telfer, a member of our team, came back from visiting one and related to us about a lady who had not been visited for nine months! It broke my heart. Our parents made great sacrifices for us and when they are old, I believe that it is our responsibility to care for them. I tell my parents to keep warm during the winter and that I will help settle any fuel bills. No parents should have to go into a home unless for medical reasons they cannot be cared for. Even then they should be visited regularly.

Discipline is vital, but it must come out of love, or it will produce a brute. However, if it is done out of love, it will produce a relationship far deeper than ever before. It seems that every time I discipline my children, our relationship and their love for me grows. More than one of my extended family (and they are in their late teens and twenties) have come to me and said, 'If I need discipline, give it to me.' One of their reasons is that some of them have never had any, and they realise as a result there is something lacking in their lives. Godly discipline, out of love, produces security in your children.

Fatherly leadership

'Then Jesus came and spoke to them saying all authority has been given to me in heaven and on earth.' (Matthew 28:18) As we have already considered in chapter three, the Lord has now delegated his authority to the husband to be the head and leader in the home. A father without authority will be weak and ineffective. While I am away from home, the children relate to Heather for everything, but the moment I walk in the door, Heather will always say in situations, 'Daddy's home now, go to him.' A father who leads will be a father who is respected by his children.

Fatherly fun and enjoyment

I believe that God wants us to have fun and a good laugh together, yet many Christian homes are intense. Psalm 2 tells us 'God in heaven laughs!' (verse 4) There is an old statement that 'The family that prays together, stays together.' However, it is equally true to say that 'The family that plays together, stays together.' Times of fun are so vital to successful family life.

Have you noticed that when the prodigal son returned home they celebrated and had a party. Our children need to be given the opportunity to have a party to celebrate from time to time. We often have a party, just for the sake of it. You don't need to wait until it is someone's birthday. How legalistic! So many Christians have the impression of God as a big man in the sky with a stick, waiting to catch us out. As fathers, we have to change this wrong concept by getting out the steak or trout or whatever and having a party every now and then!

Each month we have a family night (an undisturbed evening of fun and fellowship) where we get the candles out and have a special meal, chosen by a different member of the family each time. It usually turns out to be a great time of fun and we often end up romping on the carpet. The children so look forward to these family nights. *Fun is a key to wholeness in the family,* Yet many parents are too 'super-spiritual' or afraid of losing respect, to have fun with their family. Rather than losing respect you will gain it.

We recently had an amusing incident while reading from Proverbs during our family devotions. As we each shared what the Lord had said to us during the passage, Faith, aged 10, quoted the verse, 'A wise son brings joy to his father, but a foolish son grief to his mother.' (Proverbs 10:1) I asked her how this verse applied to her and how she could 'make her father glad,' expecting her to answer from the verse, 'by being wise and not foolish.' However, she answered, 'to play with him and tickle his feet.'

Sometimes we will go out for a slap-up meal, ten pin bowling, some wholesome theatrical or musical presentation, or even put holly in each others beds, ice cubes down each others backs or chase each other with a bucket of water! On one occasion, whilst on holiday, Peter decided to have a 'holiday' from shaving. The ladies of our family objected strongly. So with my battery razor, two held him down while another shaved him. During a recent game of 'forfeits', Heather had to put a nappy on me, while all the family watched on, (I was fully clothed at the time!)

Charades is a popular game in our family too and Peter and Stephen love water ski-ing. Over the Christmas period, the men in the family prepare supper each evening, which is quite fun! Christmas Eve is a special annual event when I make massive beefburgers which have aptly been named 'MacDoubles Beefburgers.' (The fun suggestions are unending.) Family holidays are a very precious time for us. I try to go somewhere. where we are unknown, so that I can give myself 100% to the family. Holidays are a special time for the ladies in our family as well, as the men prepare the 'brunch', (a cross between breakfast and lunch). I really count it a great privilege as a father to be able to serve the rest of the family.

Due to the wide age range in our family, we give each member of the family an opportunity to choose what they would like to do for recreation. Whatever they choose, the rest of the family become fully involved in and set their hearts to enjoy, even if it is not their 'thing'. I also seek to take each of my children out on their own from time to time. Family activities are very important, but each child also needs time with their father for themselves.

Family affection

So many people have emotional problems because they have never had a real father/child relationship. They are bottled up and unable to express their emotions because their parents were not emotionally involved with them. When our children were born, Heather would sit in bed at 6 a.m. and feed them. Then she would cuddle them and say, 'I am going to make you all cuddly.' As a result all of our children are cuddly. However, it is vital that the father gives affection too. British reserve and the tough, unemotional male mentality is breaking up many homes. God's Word tells us to 'be kindly, *affectionate* to one another with brotherly love.' (Romans 12:10) You may say, 'I can't do that,' but God's Word says that you can!

It is amazing the number of girls who have never been shown affection or had a real hug or kiss from their father, especially in their teenage years. This often leads to wrong relationships with men. When a girl falls in love with a boy, if she has not had a real relationship with her father, which includes affection, she will not know how to rightly react to love without responding sexually. Also many young people looking for love and affection, end up in immorality, because they never received godly affection. Don't be afraid to kiss your children. Six times the Bible commands us to greet each other with a holy kiss. In the church, we have subsituted God's direction to greet the brethren with a holy kiss, for a holy hug, or even just a handshake! A kiss is an intimate thing, yet a lot of people do not want to get that close. Many make the excuse that this was an Eastern custom, but you could write most of the Bible off with that same excuse if you wanted to and be left with nothing! Another excuse is to say that 'It is dangerous.' I am not naïve or unaware of this fact, but if you cannot give your daughter a holy kiss, then you are not free and need delivering. It is a very serious thing. Everything can be dangerous if misused, but that does not mean we stop relating properly.

Tears are not negative or something to be ashamed of, but positive. The Bible tells us that God puts our tears in His bottle, (Psalm 56:8) He keeps them, they are precious to Him. We are told to 'rejoice with those who rejoice, and weep with those who weep.' (Romans 12:15). Yet there are many people who are bound up emotionally because they cannot shed a few tears. Our children need to know that they can come and cry on our shoulder without any embarrassment. They never outgrow the need for fatherly affection and if there is a real relationship there, they will never feel that they are 'too big' for it, even in their teens and twenties.

Fatherly comfort

Comforting is an area that is often left to mothers. Yet Paul said, 'You know how we exhorted and comforted and charged everyone of you, *as a Father* does his own children.' (1 Thessolians 2:11) Both comforting and encouraging are important roles for any father. A child needs to know that its fathers arms are always available and that his ear is always open to them.

All fathers should be encouraging and building up their children, not just sending them off to church or Sunday school to get this done. Colossions 3:21 says, 'Fathers, do not provoke your children lest they should become discouraged.' Another meaning from the Greek for 'provoke' is to be negative with them. This will always discourage. *Always speak to build them up, never to knock them down!* Calling a child stupid, an idiot, useless, hopeless, and other names like that can seriously damage a child's security.

Fatherly provision

The Bible tells us that our heavenly Father knows the things we need, so we do not have to worry about them. He promises that as we seek first His Kingdom and righteousness, all of these things will be added unto us, (Mathew 6:32-33). 'If you then being evil know how to give good gifts to you children, how much will your Father who is in heaven give good things to those who ask Him' (Mathew 7:11). I would get the top brick off the chimney for any of my children if they needed it! If I being evil would do that, just think of our heavenly Father's goodness, 'who did not spare His own Son, but delivered Him up for us all, how shall He not, with Him also freely give us all things.' (Romans 8:32).

So many have the concept that God is stingy. I was driving down the M1 in my car a short while back, just enjoying the Lord by myself, when He spoke to me, as a father to a son. He said, 'Don, why won't you let me love you the way I want to.' My reply was 'Lord, I thought I was doing pretty well.' (I really did). But He said, 'I want to love you far more than that. You haven't really begun yet.' One of the things that He said was, 'I have given you a nice car to drive, yet when people talk to you about it, you justify having it, by saying that you need a good comfortable car because you drive 400 miles and then have to preach, and therefore need to not be tired. Also that you need a powerful car to get you around. Why don't you just say, 'my Father loves me.'

If a child

If a child lives with criticism – He learns to condemn
If a child lives with hostility – He learns to fight
If a child lives with ridicule – He learns to be shy
If a child lives with shame – He learns to feel guilt
If a child lives with tolerance – He learns to be patient
If a child lives with encouragement – He learns confidence
If a child lives with praise – He learns to appreciate
If a child lives with fairness – He learns justice
If a child lives with security – He learns to have faith
If a child lives with approval – He learns to like himself
If a child lives with acceptance and friendship – He learns to find love in the world.

14. Extended Families

'God sets the solitary in families; He brings out those who are bound in to prosperity; but the rebellious dwell in a dry land'
(Psalm 68:6).

Within each one of us there is a longing to belong. I have not met a person yet, who has not got a real longing inside to know that they belong. The largest percentage of problems that I have to deal with in counselling these days, are because deep down in people there is a sense of wanting to belong, which is not being fulfilled.

A person who is rejected will always be looking for acceptance. I used to always look for people to belong to me. I looked for my family, for my team and for my church to belong to me. When I was delivered from the bondage of rejection, I realized that I belonged to them.

We all need to know that we belong. Although I have prayed for many hundreds to be set free from the bondage or rejection and hurts, over the last 22 years in ministry, I do not believe that there can be any permanent cure from rejection unless good relationships are established.

Probably 90% of singles, widows and divorcees are lonely. Loneliness is one of the greatest diseases in the universe and also one of the most common. It is a disease in the heart, for you can be among a crowd of people and still feel lonely. *Basically, loneliness is the lack of a deep relationship with anybody.* Wives will be lonely if they have not got a deep relationship with their husbands, and husbands will be lonely if they have not got a deep relationship with their wives. You can live in the same house, sleep in the same bed, raise children together and yet still be lonely, because you have never built a genuine relationship. There are many children who are lonely because they do not have a deep relationship with their parents. Many people in the Church just shake hands with others or even hug them, but there is no building of relationships, so there is still loneliness there. Many have lost loved ones and are now left alone. So often we expect them to come and build relationships with us, they have been hurt, we need to go and build with them! It is our responsibility, (cf Acts 6:1-7). 'Pure and undefiled religion before God and the Father is this: to visit orphans and widows in their trouble, and to keep oneself unspotted from the world.' (James 1:27).

'By this all will know that you are my disciple, if you have love for one another.' (John 13:35). How we need a new infusion of God's love. This will speak louder than any preaching or open airs on street corners. Loneliness is one of the world's worst conditions. It is painful, and causes all kinds of problems. It is the churches responsibility to care for all these groups of people, not the state's! It is our fault if they remain lonely after we realize their condition.

Loneliness should not be a problem in a Church that is really relating together. When our churches are properly structured, everyone will be cared for. I believe that extended families are a major way for this to be worked out. Everyone needs to be loved and it is not sufficient to say to someone 'God loves you'; we need to be the love of God to them. The Bible tells us that it is hypocritical saying to someone, 'be warmed and be filled', yet doing nothing practical about it.

Genesis 2:18 says, 'It is not good that man should be alone'. It is in 'families', that God sets the 'solitary'. (Ps. 68:6). Jesus believed in extended families. One the cross He looked at his mother, then He looked at John, the disciple He loved, and said, 'Woman, behold your son.

Son, behold your mother.' And from that day, his disciple 'took her into his own home'. She became part of his family. (John 19:26).

I am a great believer in extended families. Recently we had some extra rooms built onto our house so that the family could increase in number. I honestly believe that there is no better answer for today's generation. There are so many who have never really known the love of their parents and need a family where they know that they belong.

Those in my extended family have the same place in my heart as my own children. They are not treated differently. I don't believe in lodgers. If any of my extended family are hurt or ill, then I am emotionally affected. Why? Because God has given them to me. I would not take any one into my family just out of sympathy. I have got to know that God has given them to me. He gave me my children in the flesh, but He gave me my extended family as well. *It was only the method of giving them that was different*. If God has given them, how can there be any difference? The Scriptures tell us that 'The alien living with you *must be treated as one of your native born*. Love him as yourself, for you were aliens in Egypt. I am the Lord your God.' (Leviticus 19:34) There is no scriptural ground for treating the extended family differently. In fact, we do not like using the words 'extended family' now, because we are just family.

There is such a lack of fathers in God, will you be one? Everyone needs a family they can relate to, where they know that they are loved and feel a part of, even if it is not possible to live under the same roof. The person who lives in a flat needs to relate to a family. The door needs to be open to them, so they feel welcome and part of the family. They need to have their own key, so that they can come when they want, without feeling like intruders. It is here that loneliness can be dealt with.

As Frances, a member of my extended family, puts it, 'I know that the relationships which I am building within the family are going to last for eternity, they are not just something until I get married, they are forever. I know that I am loved, cared for, needed and wanted for who I am within the family.'

I believe that it is God's best that everyone should be relating to a family. Do not misunderstand me and immediately take a dozen people into your home, saying, 'God said I am going to be a father to them'. Get your relationships right with your own children first, then let God add to the family one at a time, working things out with them before you take any others in. But I challenge you; if God has given you a home, don't be selfish with it; share it. It will give you unspeakable joy.

Those who have come to live in our family have enriched the children rather than taken away from them. My children could not imagine life without the precious people God has given us.

Taking the initiative

It is very important that the whole family is involved in the initiation of any new people. If just one or two, the parents or even the majority invite someone in, without the families full consent, you may well end up with your own children getting hurt, becoming resentful or feeling that they are losing out. In the past we have set aside time as a family to pray and share together before coming to any agreement as to whether it is right to receive someone into the family or not. If we are not all convinced that God is giving the person to us, then the answer must be 'No'.

A good example was when Peter came to join the team and moved down to Cornwall. Heather and I felt that it was right for him to be in our family, but in practical terms there was no way that he could, because there were no spare bedrooms. When we got together as a family and talked it through, Stephen who was 13 years old at the time immediately said, 'He can share my room.' Because of that it was an indication that it was right for Peter to join us.

Sometimes, the reason for extended family is simply geographical, for example when people move away from their parents for work or college reasons. There are also casualties of today's society, like broken homes. These are the kind of people that are possibilities for God to call into an extended family situation. It is not right for every person to get a flat, especially if they have never worked out true family relationships. I believe that this has been the cause of some shipwrecked marriages, for marriage is not the best situation to work out your first good relationship. I have deliberately sought to avoid presenting this subject in a mechanical, 'This is the way to do it' style, for each situation will be very different, and will need to be worked out in life. Some people have opened their homes under pressure or because they felt sorry for a person. Compassion if vital, but does not constitute a call. You must hear from God and know in your heart that it is right to take a person into your family.

Because people have been hurt in the past, they often wear a mask seeking to hide their real self lest they get hurt again. Before they are willing to take off their mask and let you into the innermost secrets of their hearts, they have to be satisfied that you really love them and can be trusted.

This takes time, but it is only then that you can minister the Lord's healing to them and begin to build genuine relationships.

Taking someone new into your home can be painful as they may well have been used to doing things in ways unacceptable to the family. Therefore, their first reactions to discipline may be quite stormy.

On occasions, we have had to meet together as a family to face certain issues. On one such occasion, we had to strongly confront a new member who had sinned and not owned up to it. They came to the place where they admitted their sin, and made restitution. Immediately there was tremendous love flowing from the family to that person. It actually brought more security to them and in the end because they discovered that nothing they could do would change the family's commitment to them.

Whatever we discovered about them we would still love and accept them. We are accepted in the beloved. Jesus accepted us when we were totally wrong and the same principle applies in family life.

Relating to step-children

Finally, in today's society it is common for families to include step children. In that situation it is vitally important that the partner who does not have a blood relationship with the children, *must* receive them as their own flesh and blood and get beyond ever thinking of them as step children. It is sad to hear such statements as, 'That is your child.' We must get beyond thinking of them as step-children and receive them as 'our' children. They are a part of the husband or wife you love, so get to know them and love them.

Two of our children were step-children to Heather. Nigel was eight and Julia was five years old when Heather and I married. However, the Lord made it very easy for us, as shortly before they came to live with us permanently, Jean Darnell, unaware of the move, gave Heather a prophecy that God was giving her something to look after for Him. Your children are a gift from God to you. The method by which He gave them does not matter. They may be step-children, adopted, natural born or extended family but see them as God's gift to you.

As Heather once put it, 'Nigel and Julia are two of my best friends. Before I had any authority into their lives in the area of discipline or training, I went out to be a friend to them.

We need to realize that step-children will probably need to build a fresh trust in adults. Many will feel betrayed and bitter or resentful, so be sensitive to them.'

The fact that Heather was looking after Nigel and Julia for the Lord was a great encouragement to her and brought such a commitment that she rarely travelled with me until they were married and off our hands. Only then did she feel free to accompany me more often.

Teach your own children how to relate to them. When Joel was seven, the class at school had to cut out pictures of people and write the names of their families down under neath them. His teacher, looking quite surprised, said, 'You cannot possibly have all those brothers and sisters.' But Joel was convinced that he had! After Heather and I, Nigel and Julia were the first brothers and sisters he put down, then Francis, then Stephen, Faith and the other extended family! The amusing thing was that he called them all'Double' and there were nine of us living in the home at that time, not including Nigel and Julia who were both married by then!

15. Singled Out

(Peter)

The subject of singles is such a vast one for it includes single young people, single older people, those who have never met the right person, those who are not called to marry, those who are preparing to get married and others who are widowed or divorced. Therefore, I want to share some principles that apply to each of these groups and to honestly look at some of the blessings and some of the problems that come to us as singles.

One of the first things we need to see is that being single is not weird. After all, everyone is single at some time. Being single is an important time in any person's life and one that should not be wasted. It can also be a time where we can know fulfilment.

Yet there are often external pressures from those around who make such 'comforting' statements as, 'You singles can be as happy as normal people.' Or 'How come a nice person like you is not married?' Such comments are often hurtful, leaving the recipient feeling like a second-class citizen or even an ogre, abnormal, or at best, 'half a person'. Others have been pressurized into acting hastily, making decisions they have later regretted, motivated by such comments as 'He is such a lovely boy, he would make a great husband', or 'You don't know what you are missing.' We need to be careful to avoid making insensitive comments to other.

As well as the external pressures, many are attacked by the internal pressure of such thoughts as, 'I may be left on the shelf, I am nearly seventeen and I don't have a boyfriend or girlfriend.'

'Oh no, I have found another grey hair.'
'I might never meet anyone else.'

The statement 'God told me we should marry,' is fine as long as there is a mutual and naturally growing love between a couple. However, many have been put under pressure by this comment. The number of times I have heard those word spoken to me implies that either God believes in bigamy or people have got their guidance wrong!

There is nothing strange about being single. 25% of all male adults in the U.S.A. are single and 35% of all adult females (a great comfort to those living in England.)

Jesus was single and fulfilled. He did not say of the Christian, 'I have come that you might have life and have it more abundantly, *as long as you are married.*' It is possible in whatever state we are to be content. Paul was single, yet he too was fulfilled. In fact, many of the biblical characters most mightily used by God, like Elijah, Elisha and John the Baptist, were single.

There are advantages to being single, especially a greater release to do God's work. You do not have the same ties on your time or finances either. (See 1 Corinthians 7:25-35) For 'he who is unmarried cares for the things that belong to the Lord, how he may please the Lord' (1 Corinthians 7:32). Therefore, such an opportunity can be used to eternal benefit laying up treasures in heaven. It is not second best.

The best is to be in the will of God for you at the present time.

Living in the present

Many singles either live in the future or in the past. They regard singlehood as a necessary evil while they await their prince (or princess) to ride along on their white horse and rush them off to their castle where they live 'happily ever after.' They live continually in the future, drifting from day to day, singing, 'one day my prince will come.' It has been suggested that a suitable hymn for the Women's Guild theme song, would be, 'I want a man, I want a man, I want a mansion in the sky.'

Someone once described this as the 'waiting room mentality'. Where people sit on the edge of their chair wondering if they are the next whose name will be called out. Only to be disheartened, as someone else gets to see the doctor first. For some, they sit in fear, wondering, 'Am I going to get in to see the doctor? I will probably be dead by the time it is my turn'.

I remember at the age of 14 saying to one of my younger friends who came round to 'play' with me, 'You have got to realize it is fine me spending time playing with you now, but I will probably be married in two years time!' (Obviously not the word of a prophet.)

There are many others who constantly live in the past, meditating upon how they nearly married and what could have been. Either state of mind prevents us from relating to the present. Such attitudes usually stifle any relationship with God too. It is no accident that you are single now.

Enjoy Him forever

There is nothing more exciting than living all out for the Lord. We were made by God for a relationship with Him. The Westminster Shorter Catechism says that the chief aim of man is to 'glorify God and to enjoy Him forever.' We need to see that a relationship with God is not something to tide us over until we can get a partner. Though marriage is ordained and blessed by God, divorce statistics show that it is not the answer to all life's problems. I am not pretending, or even suggesting that being single has always been easy for me. There have been times when I have felt lonely, and other times when I would have loved to have a wife and family. However, my primary source of fulfilment comes from my relationship with God.

No human relationship can fulfil one totally. In fact, it

is quite amusing listening first to singles saying, 'If only I were married, I would be fulfilled', then a few minutes later hearing a married person say, 'It is okay for singles; they have an easy time.' (Don't we have short memories?)

To be or not to be?

Marriage is certainly the usual pattern for life. In general, it is God's will that 'a man shall leave his father and mother and be joined to his wife, and they shall become one flesh' (Genesis 2:24). Even with Adam, enjoying a perfect relationship with God in an unfallen state, God said, 'It is not good that man should be alone, I will make a helper compatable to him.' (Gen 2v 18)

'He who finds a wife finds a good thing, and obtains favour from the Lord' (Proverbs 18:22). The apostle Paul was not anti-marriage as some would suggest (1 Timothy 5v 14). Although his personal feeling was that 'It is good for a man not to touch a woman' (1 Corinthians 7:1), he went on to say, 'Nevertheless, because of sexual immorality, let each man have his own wife, and let each woman have her own husband' (1 Cor 7:2). 'To the unmarried, and to the widows, it is good for them if they remain even as I am, but if they cannot exercise self-control, let them marry for it is better for them to marry than to burn with passion' (1 Corinthians 7:7 & 8). The key to 1 Corinthians chapter 7 is the statement in verse 7 that, 'Each one has his own *gift* from God, one in this manner, and another in that'. 'As God has distributed to each one, so let Him walk' (1 Corinthians 7:17). The key is our proper gifting. God has called some to celibacy. 'For there are eunuchs who were born thus from their mothers' womb, and there are eunuchs who were made eunuchs by men, and there are eunuchs who have made themselves eunuchs for the Kingdon of Heaven's sake. He who is able to accept it, let him accept it' (Mathew 19:12). When someone is called to be celibate, they will not have a driving desire to marry and will be content to remain single. Though marriage is the usual pattern for life, it is not the only one. However, Jesus said, 'All cannot accept this saying, but only those to whom it has been given' (Mathew 19:11). Therefore, it is fair to assume that there is no need to fear that you have been called to celibacy. If it is your gifting from God, you will be able to accept it with ease, and without undue pressure or a constant desire to marry, but will be fully satisfied as a single.

In the Lord

Notice that when Paul refers to marrying in 1 Corinthians chapter 7 he makes the condition that any partner must be 'in the Lord' (1 Corinthians 7:39 & 1 Timothy 5:5). The Scriptures are very clear that a Christian should only marry another Christian. The Bible clearly condemns being 'unequally yoked with an unbeliever' (2 Corinthians 6:14),

'Do not be unequally yoked together with unbelievers, for what fellowship has righteousness with lawlessness? And what communion has light with darkness? Or what part has a believer with an unbeliever. And what agreement has the temple of God with idols? For you are the temple of the living God.'

The term to be 'yoked', referred to two oxen who wore the same yoke so that they could pull in the same direction, and thus be more effective. But when for a Christian and non-Christian yoke themselves together, this creates all kinds of problems because they are going in different directions. Christians and non-Christians live in two completely different kingdoms and see things from completely different angles. The Christian wants to see godly discipline brought to their children. However, for the non-Christian, discipline will most likely be out of anger, or non-existent. The Christian wants to give to the Lord and pay their tithe. However, the non-Christian will see this as a complete waste of money. Most non-Christians see reading their horoscopes and other occult practices, as 'innocent fun'. However, the Christian realizes how dangerous these things are. For the non-Christian resentment is acceptable with the excuse that the other person 'deserves it.' However, the Christian realizes that they must forgive. We could go on looking at other areas. But basically, there is a clash of priorities and of direction in the area of friends, morality, vocation, family roles etc. Where two animals are 'yoked' together, pulling in the same direction, there is tremendous strength. However, if they are pulling in opposite directions the trauma and pain involved requires little imagination.

I have known those who claimed that they went out with a non-Christian to 'witness to them', in the hope of winning them for the Lord. Such a consideration is extremely naïve. In almost all the many cases I have known where people have done this, rather than the unbeliever being won for the Lord, the believer has backslidden. What does the occasional 'success' prove? That God is merciful even when a person has disobeyed him. If God tells us not to be unequally yoked, which includes any strong binding relationship, we cannot expect His blessing on our disobedience. The Maker's Instructions are clear and there are no exceptions to the rule. Even of the few cases where I have known the unbeliever to be converted, it has usually been to please their partner, and on marriage, almost without exception, they have backslidden. I would include in 'unequally yoked', any who are not going on with God or willing to move into the things that God is calling them to. They will hold their partner back.

Even as I write this chapter a letter has arrived seeking advice from yet another dear saint who married a non-Christian. She says, 'I was a Christian when I married, but loved my husband dearly and could not bear being parted from him.' She went on to share the problems she had experienced since then and said, 'I suffered a nervous breakdown three years ago because I felt continually pulled in two directions.' I share this, not to condemn anyone who finds themselves in this situation but to warn any contemplating a similar course of action! When God gives directions for our life, it is not to rob us, or to stop us enjoying ourselves. It is for our good. He wants us to enjoy life to the full. However, if we want the best in life, we need to follow the Maker's Instructions.

One girl I knew quite well, began to go out with a non-Christian, although she knew clearly what the Word of God said. I warned her, but she replied, 'He is close to the kingdom.' She later wrote to me saying that he had become a Christian and she was now going to marry him. About six months later, I saw her mother and said, 'How is their marriage going?' To which she replied, 'It is terrible. He appeared to walk with the Lord until he had married her. Then, when he had got what he wanted, he just dropped Christianity and has stopped her going to Church meetings too. Her life is a misery.' Although it is sad, she can blame no-one but herself.

We can however, repent and get into a place where God can turn that situation to good. Even then it is vital to see, that, although God will forgive us, we often have to live with the consequences of our sin. If you murder someone, God will forgive you, if you truly repent, but asking for forgiveness does not instantly raise the person you murdered from the dead, If a girl gets pregnant outside of marriage God can forgive her, but that does not immediately get rid of the child.

You are special

We need to see that God made us for a relationship with Him and wants us to enjoy fulfilment. He called us by name. God said, 'Peter, I have chosen you. I want you' (John 15:16). He cares for each one of us personally even in the minutest of details. Even the hairs of your head are numbered' (Matt 10v 30). There is no-one alive quite like you! You are special; you are unique! One of our greatest needs is to accept ourselves as we are. We should be able to look at ourselves in the mirror (a full length one) and say 'I accept this body, Lord, and thank you for it.'

This of course, is not an excuse for being five stone overweight or for misusing our bodies in other ways. We have been made stewards of all that we are and have and are accountable to God in looking after these things. However, it is vital that we can accept our talents and develop them, and also accept our limitations. When God made you, He did not make a mistake! I love the Scripture in Ephesians 2:10 where it tells us that we are 'His workmanship, created in Christ Jesus for good works.' The Jerusalemn Bible describes us as 'God's work of art.' Be thankful for the body that God has given you. *You are God's work of art!*

16. Four Keys To Fulfilment As Singles

(Peter)

If we will surrender ourselves and our will to the Lord, we will make a lot less mistakes and miss a lot of heartache! So let us now consider four important keys to fulfilment as singles.

1. Trust the Lord

Whether you are to marry or not, the best preparation is a total commitment to the Lord. You can trust Him. God knows what He is doing! Very often it is this area of choosing a partner where people say, 'This my department Lord'. They have some misguided idea that if God chooses a partner, He is going to choose someone who looks like the 'back of a bus'. This is a sad picture of God. He is our Father, Abba, Daddy. God wants the best for you! If your choice didn't work out in the past, don't worry, God has got someone better.

It is important to realize that God knows what our desires and needs will be ten and twenty years from now, we don't. When I consider some of the people who I had 'crushes' on in the past, I am so grateful that I did not marry them. It would have been disastrous. God knows best. He knows the end from the beginning. He is already in the 21st century! He knows what your needs are going to be throughout your whole life. That is why we are told to, 'Seek first the Kingdom of God, and His righteousness, and all these things shall be added to you' (Matthew 6:33). As we seek first His Kingdom, all our needs will be met. This should bring a tremendous security and prevent us from worrying about our lives (Mathew 6:25). We are to seek first the Kingdom of God, not to seek first a partner, then all these things will be added to us. Some young singles are unable to relate properly to the opposite sex, simply, because in the back of their mind there is the constant thought, 'Is this the one for me?' Despite the image portrayed by the media that a couple, 'fall in love', this is not always the case. Often marriages result from natural growing friendships.

Rebecca was a beautiful girl who would have had no trouble in finding a boyfriend. Yet we read in the Word of God that she was happy serving her father and her family, trusting God. Because she was seeking first the Kingdom, the Lord made sure that she 'happened' to be at the right well, at the right time, to meet the right man. As we seek first His Kingdom, God can make sure that you are at the 'right well' at the right time. It is a tremendous relief to be able to walk down the street without wondering if you have just missed your life-time partner! God can make sure that you are in the right place at the right time. It is also a tremendous comfort to realize that the Lord knows how we feel. In His humanity there may have been times when Jesus desired to settle down and marry. He was also subjected to the sexual temptations that you are too, because the Bible tells us that He was tempted in all points as we are, but without sin (Heb. 4:15). He knows what you are going through, so feel free to talk to Him about them.

When we are walking with God, letting Him shape our lives, we can rest assured that He is in control. The Bible does not say, 'Thou shalt marry by seventeen' or 'If thou art not married by twenty-six, thou art upon the shelf for the rest of thy life.' You can trust him. Let the Lord deal with any issues in your life so that you do not hold up His purpose and plans for you.

2. Avoid unholiness

We live in a world where there is great pressure to

compromise. God has given us a free will and therefore, when we are tempted, we are faced with a choice, whether to obey Him or to sin. It is an important choice, for, 'Whatever a man sows, that also shall he reap' (Galatians 6:7). Sin always pays wages.

Our emotions are very powerful driving forces. However, they are not of the devil; God has given them to us. Nevertheless, we are faced with a choice as to whether we learn to control them, or let them run riot and dominate our lives which we will later regret. In many ways the period of singleness is a time that God gives us to learn to say 'no'. It is vital that a man learns to control himself before he is married.

Although God can forgive us if we fall, many people live with regrets. We cannot turn our life back.

The sexual drive is one of the strongest urges that God has given us. In the bounds of a life-time husband/wife relationship it is beautiful and given as a blessing. There is nothing wrong with sexual desire. It is as natural as the desire for food or sleep. However, it is important that we learn to rightly control this urge. Many young people with great potential for God's service have ruined their lives by doing their own thing in this area. There is forgiveness, cleansing and restoration if a person has fallen sexually, and God can cleanse that person so that they are as pure as any virgin. However, *the greatest wedding present* partners can give each other, is the knowledge that they are the 'one and only' and that they have kept themselves wholly for each other. There is something very beautiful and precious about this. Sin is pleasurable, however it always reaps results.

The main area we need to learn to control is not our actions but our thoughts. The well known saying that 'the devil finds work for idle hands' extends to idle minds too. We are the temple of the Holy Spirit (1 Cor. 6:18-20). Therefore 'flee sexual immortality. Every sin that man does is outside of the body, but he who commits sexual immorality sins against his own body. Do you not know that your body is the temple of the Holy Spirit, who is in you, whom you have from God and you are not your own? For you were bought at a price, therefore glorify God in your body and in your spirit, which atre God's' (Corinthians 6:19-20). I have shared in more detail on this aspect of living in victory in my book *Battle Stations*. (Published by Kingsway).

We have passions that are easily aroused. Therefore, it is necessary to avoid the things that are going to pull us down and tempt us. Philippians 4:8 is a good guideline for anything we are about to do, read, or watch on T.V. 'Whatever things are true, whatever things are noble, whatever things are just, whatever things are pure, whatever things are lovely, whatever things are of good report, if there is any virtue and if there is anything praise-worthy, meditate on these things'.

David the Psalmist asked the question, 'How can a young man keep his way pure?' Then he answered it, 'By living according to your word. I seek you with all my heart; do not let me stray from your commands. I have hidden your word in my heart, that I might not sin against you' (Psalm 119:9-11). On many occasions, I have prayed, 'Lord keep me during times of weakness'. It has been great to see how God in His grace has kept me and protected me from many awkward situations. Do you want to stay holy? If you do, you will. If you find that you have a bondage in some area or feel that it is too hard to stand in victory, seek prayer that you might be set free. Decide now that you are not going to compromise. God knows best. Sin always leads to regrets.

Dress is an area where many Christians compromise. Seeking for a partner, they dress, behave, speak and live in a way that will turn others on and lower their standards. Yet they would say, 'I want to have a godly partner.' Yet a godly partner would not give them a second look. If you want a godly partner, live a godly life. Flirting hurts people. I believe that to lead someone on, giving the impression that you are interested in building a relationship, when you really do not intend to, is sin.

3. Avoid independence

Having made this statement, do not misunderstand me; I am not suggesting that we should fail to discover who we are, or lack confidence, but that we should avoid withdrawal, selfishness and failing to discover our importance in the family.

(a) Withdrawal. There will be times when we need the help of others. Times when we need to open up and share with those we can trust. It is easy to withdraw saying, 'No-one else will understand what I am going through.' However, the Bible says that we are all tempted in a like manner (1 Cor. 10:13). Satan doesn't even have a new book of tricks for ministers! If you do not learn to open up before you are married, it will not be any easier afterwards. We all need those whom we can share with, laugh with, cry with, and go to at any time and share what we are going through, knowing that they will have a listening ear and help us see things in perspective.

Have you noticed when facing a problem on your own, how easy it is to see things out of perspective? I remember going to Don on a particular issue which looked so massive to me, that I could not see any way out. I wept as I shared with him. Yet, after I had finished talking, he said, 'That is no problem', and within minutes had destroyed my whole argument. What had appeared so massive to me on my own, came into perspective as I shared it. Problems are so much bigger when you keep them to yourself. There is much truth in the statement that, 'A problem shared is a problem halved'.

It is common for people who are hurt and rejected to seek consolation from a pet or even a teddy bear or doll, rather than sharing with someone who can really help them. This leads to a very unreal world, as teddies do not tell lies, but neither do they tell us the truth. We need people who we can share with and open our heart up to. Many bottle up their emotions and are unable to give or receive love. They need setting free in Jesus' name.

The Bible says that Jesus wept publicly at Lazarus' tomb. I can imagine those around saying, 'Jesus isn't taking it very well. What we are going to do. I hope He doesn't have a nervous breakdown.' Jesus did not bottle up his emotions. There is nothing unmanly about crying, rather there is something healthy about being able to cry.

God never intended us to be lonely or isolated. We all need human love. The Bible tells us that God has set the solitary in families (Psalm 68:6). I believe, wherever possible we should avoid living on our own. It is a great temptation for someone in their late teens or early twenties who wants to find their own feet, to move from their home and get a flat. University also seems a grand opportunity to be their 'own boss', without having parents to bring direction or say what time they should be in at night. Yet so many Christians go off the rails when they get to University because they become independent. Even if it is not possible to live with a family, you still need to relate to one, which you can feel a part of. There is no need to be alone. Ask God to give you such a family. We all need human love; God made us that way (Genesis 22:18). In one sense, Adam was not alone; he had God. However, even Adam needed more than just his relationship with God

(b) Selfishness. This becomes a problem with many at college as they become their own boss. They can get up when they like and do whatever they like, whenever they like. To be in a place where you have no-one to consult in the things you do, how to spend your money and use your time is dangerous. It is not too hard to imagine the problems that often result when two independent people, fresh from college get married! There will be few problems in a marriage if it involves two unselfish people, who are seeking their partner's good.

(c) Failing to discover your importance in the family. Sisters are prone to a feeling of inferiority and a lack of worth and need their brothers to let them know how important they are to them. Stephen and I seek to take the single girls in the family out for a meal until they get a boyfriend to do it.

In fact, they took me out for a 'Wimpy' a little while back (the little one is ten), which was such a blessing. Let them know how important they are. Stand by them and care for them.

As Stephen once said when talking about family, concerning sisters, 'Play around with them, but be sensitive. Don't be too rough. Treat them as ladies, especially when they are growing up and in their teenage years. Start to protect them. If your sister is going somewhere at night, walk her there. If you have got a car, drive her there, (if she trusts you to drive). If she hasn't got a boyfriend, take her out for a meal every now and then. Little things like this show that you love them.'

Family involvement is an important part of maturing. Yet many teenagers see it as a burden or hindrance to their development and freedom. Sadly, some become no more than lodgers, making no contribution to family life and cutting themselves off from genuine input. There is a temptation during teenage years to think that you have 'arrived' and outgrown the usefulness of your parents, brothers and sisters. This reaction is quite common. However, realize that parents and older brothers and sisters have gone through this stage and have come out the other side with a greater wisdom and insight from which much can be learned. What better place to learn such things as patience, sharing, co-operation, forgiveness, adaptability, acceptance and self-giving, than in the family?

Sisters can be an important 'tool' in learning how to handle the varying emotional changes that occur in a woman's menstrual cycle. Being brought up in family without sisters, I found it hard to relate to the varying emotional cycles girls experience.

Being an emotionally level person, I was thrown by how women could react differently at certain times of the month, and therefore, occasionally, I reacted insensitively. Being involved since in a family with a number of women at various stages of development has helped me greatly in learning to be sensitive when I notice a reaction that is out of character. This is not to excuse moodiness or depression, as I have also seen Christ's victory over the curse manifest in their lives (see Chapter 5).

Brothers can also be an important 'tool' as a girl learns how to relate to other men in her life. Natural non-sexual relationships in a healthy family environment, teach a girl to enjoy the company of men. You can also learn how to hold conversation on various topics, not just 'women's subjects'. You can also encourage them in the development of their leadership potential by allowing them to take responsibility for you. This will not only develop their character but yours too.

4. Avoid aimlessness

(a). Don't waste your time. It is so easy to live in a Sleeping Beauty type daze, waiting for Prince Charming to come along. Many others who have lost their parents, or had a relationship break up live constantly thinking of what might have been. So often the past becomes the enemy of the present.

Many are held back by failures of the past and thus become aimless. The Lord can heal the hurts in your heart and help you to adjust. Talk these through with the Lord. He is not going to be shocked if you share your heart. He knows how you feel anyway. God is interested and He won't be offended, so be honest. So many people live in self pity and negativism. Such people are awful company. *We need to come to the place where we do not feel sorry for ourselves.* This is selfishness and we should repent of such an attitude. It is also easy to be overwhelmed by the feeling of, 'If only I had . . . . it would be different.' The past is gone and we must rest in God's forgiveness, love and sovereignty. Give to the Lord your regrets, your guilt, and your failings. He really is a sovereign God. Receive the Lord's forgiveness and forgive any from the past who have hurt you. We can all think of things that we now regret. Let us not live on past regrets, but move on to new things with God.

b. Be creative. God is a creative God and we are made in His image. Satan is not creative, but we are. Have you ever thought that in the depths of the ocean there are beautiful flowers that no human eye has ever seen? Only God enjoys their beauty. (As I look around the countryside, I often think He must like the colour green!) We can be creative in our dress, but still godly, clean, tidy and attractive. Yet many Christians write others off if they do not fit into their little compartment. For some Christians, their only concept is wearing black suits, or clothes out of the 18th century. We need to take care of our appearance. Many Christians let themselves go and say such things as, 'I have waited all this time for a husband, so I am never going to get one', ceasing to take care in having their hair done attractively and dressing beautifully. As someone once put it, 'The Lord would have a hard job convincing me to marry them if they were His choice for me.' Men should take care that they dress and smell attractively. Ladies can learn how to use make-up, not to hide what is really there, but to be creative, and to develop what God has made them.

c. Singleness is the time to prepare for marriage. We should seek to be the best that we can be. Have a goal that you will be the best husband or the best wife for your partner. Many singles are lazy, avoiding practical jobs like the washing up etc. We need to change in these areas now, even if we do not like the idea. Life is not just doing the things we feel like doing. We are not called to live in the realm of our feelings. Much of life we might not enjoy naturally. However, if our attitude is right, we can learn to enjoy everything.

Men should seek to be masculine and learn to be decisive, men of their word, men who can handle finance. They should deal with laziness in their life and be hard-working. Girls should be feminine and learn how to look after children, change nappies, cook, sew etc . . . They should learn how to love and to serve. If both partners go into the marriage as servants, it will cut down a lot of the problems. Learn to look out for things to do and then get on with them. Learn to be a servant. Seek to get your life sorted out, letting God deal with any issues or areas in your life. Let Him deal with any moodiness or bad tempered-ness. If you are lazy now, you will regret it later. For 'Slothfulness casts one into a deep sleep, and an idle person will suffer hunger' (Prov. 19:15). Set yourself the goal, to be the best for the Lord!

If you have never been filled with the Holy Spirit, seek for the Lord to fill you. The Holy Spirit is our 'comforter' (John 14:16). In the Greek that is, 'One sent alongside to help'. The Holy Spirit comes to help and strengthen you at your points of need. He is the 'Holy Spirit' and comes to bring His holiness into our lives.

God has a purpose for you that is specific. Your relationship with the Lord needs to be top priority. Seek first His Kingdom, and to live for His glory and He will then provide for those other needs.

17. Preparation For Marriage

Several people have requested that we include in this book the teaching I give to couples preparing for marriage.

I usually have six separate sessions leading up to the marriage date, where teaching and instructions are given. The couple are encouraged to pray and discuss these before the next session, which often begins with questions concerning the last one and a sharing of the decisions which they have made.

On occasions, during counselling of married couples, some have commented that if they had been given proper counselling and taught the principles of God's word before they married, it would have saved them from a lot of heartaches and problems.

In view of these facts I have written these sessions in the same strain as I would share them with a couple preparing for marriage.

1. The Wedding

a. Planning the Wedding Day. Any old thing will not do. The wedding day should be very memorable – a day that will bring pleasant memories and be a strong influence upon you for the rest of your lives together.

The bridegroom-to-be, should fully understand that it is the bride's 'big day'. Therefore, he should do everything he can to make it a wonderful day for her. Both the bride and the bridegroom should begin to plan, pray and share their desires for the day *together*. It should be an exciting time as they go shopping and share together in making decisions about the wedding.

Include – Wedding present list
Bridesmaids – how many? who? what type and colour or dresses?
Type of service
Order of service
Hymns
Who should participate in the actual marriage service?
Who would you like to share and speak at the reception?
What kind of reception is it to be and who do you invite?
Should you take Holy Communion together during the service?
Whether to have it tape recorded or video'd etc

It is also important to arrange for a very good photographer and to believe that you will have a really good album to remember the day by.

As an act of love, in seeking to please the groom, it is good for the bride to discreetly discover what type of dress he really likes, (eg: lace, brocade, cotton, long or short, should the veil be long or short? etc.) In the same way, the groom should discover the type of suit the bride likes.

b. Planning the Honeymoon I believe it is good to have the best honeymoon possible, even if it means a sacrifice. I am aware the personal desires for different types of honeymoons persist, but I also believe every honeymoon, wherever possible, should be in a warm climate, in a hotel where you can relax easily, and where you are unlikely to meet anybody you know, so that you can really be on your own and able to get to know each other in depth.

On your return, it is advisable, if possible to have an additional week in your new home so that you can learn to live together before going back to work.

The honeymoon should be approached in the right frame of mind, positively, believing that you are going to thoroughly enjoy and receive the best from it.

c. Planning the New Home The Bible teaches the sanctity

of the family. Therefore I believe every married couple should share their life together in a home of their own, however simple it might be, even if it is only two rooms.

'For this reason a man shall leave his father and mother and be joined to his wife and the two shall become one flesh' (Eph 5:31).

When you are married, you leave your father and mother (your parents must also let you go), to begin a new life together with the husband as the head of the home and the wife in submission to him.

It is so essential that you start your life on your own, away from in-laws. You should seriously consider postponing the wedding if you are unable to find somewhere on your own immediately.

A true home is somewhere where there is love. It is far more than bricks and furniture. You will find yourselves able to express your love to each other in a far more wonderful way as you begin life together. Use your time together to the maximum, to pray and share together, building good, solid and deep foundation in your relationships, so that it is unshakeable when pressures come along.

2. Relationships

Many times as I counsel young couples on this vital subject they have smiled at me disbelievingly. One of the most important things to realize is that, as yet, you do not really know each other, no matter how long you have been courting, you still do not really *know* one another.

I know of some couples who have been courting for years (one such couple for seven years), who really thought they knew each other well until they had been married for a few months. No-one can really know another until they have begun to live together. There are still many things to discover about each other.

Keep your relationship clean, keep right with God and each other. Keep short accounts with God and ask each other for forgiveness whenever it is necessary, *as soon as possible*.

It is vital that you do not get married with the idea that you are going to change each other. Unless you can love each other *now*, just as you see each other, being prepared to love *whatever* you discover about your partner, I would seriously suggest that you call the marriage off before it is too late.

You must be willing to accept each other as you are.

It is so important to share your hearts at the very deepest level, being open and not wearing a mask or trying to be someone else. Perhaps you have a picture in your mind of the kind of person you think your partner would really like to have married and so you try to live like that image. This will not work – be yourself.

It is important before the wedding day to regularly pray, seek God and read His Word together. In doing this, you will discover that you are not just going to be one flesh after your marriage, but also one spirit. Endeavour to have the same spiritual desires and hunger for God in your lives so that you can both pull in the same direction.

The Bible teaches that we should not be unequally yoked. However, I believe that it is equally important not to become unequally yoked *after* marriage. Together, you must both seek to go on with God, hungry and thirsty for the Lord, with the same spiritual desires at all times.

Again I would emphasize the importance of playing your correct role in the family. The Maker's Instructions are clear, and guarantee the best results! For example, I say to the prospective wife, if she cannot respect herself and submit to her future husband, then it is best if they do not marry.

3. Economics

Finance has been at the root of many marriage problems and the cause of some breaking up. Therefore it is important to plan and talk through on this subject long before you are married. It is essential for you to hold the same goals economically.

A saying that is often quoted is 'when the bills come in

through the door, love flies out through the window.' Undue pressures can come into your marriage relationships because of finance. It is better to go without some items of furniture than to have hire purchase repayments, which can bring pressures upon the financial position of the home. There is tremendous joy to be received through saving up for an item and then going together to buy it, paying cash (and very likely receiving a good cash discount), far more than having everything at once on HP. (Often, by the time it is paid for, it is worn out or at the best in a second hand condition. In addition, you will be paying a high interest.) For example, it would be better to go without a television set than to have it on HP and find pressure in paying the instalments or rental. In fact, I strongly advise couples not to have a television set in the first year of their married life. It can be such a hindrance to sharing together and building a good strong relationship.

A mortgage for a house, I believe, is acceptable, because you do not really own the house until it has been totally paid for. (The building society hold the deeds and therefore this is not really much different from paying a rent to a local council or landlord.) it is essential to plan on what you can and what you cannot afford. Live well within your means, so that you have spare cash to live with comfortably each week.

It is also very important to see that when you are married every part of you should become one. 'This includes your finances. Many problems are caused in marriage by the husband saying, 'This is mine' and the wife retaliating with, 'That is mine.' When we marry it should become *our* money. There should be only one account and that being a joint account of husband and wife. Sadly, where this principle has not been established, I have seen legacies destory marriages. You are one now and whatever you have and receive automatically becomes 'ours'.

Independence was the first sin. It is still sin, yet our modern society tends to teach independence in marriage, which is very destructive.

4. Sexual relationships

This is a vital part of any marriage relationship and rightly so. Most couples preparing for marriage are looking forward to this aspect very much indeed. God created sexual relationships as part of His plan for our lives. Therefore, within marriage it is wholesome and good. The husband needs to realize that it is his responsibility to satisfy his wife and bring her to a full climax also. The wife should similarly seek to fully satisfy her husband and make this her main motive in the relationship. In sexual relationships, selfishness is sin and destructive. Whether it is being demanding or unresponsive, both are a display of selfishness.

Intercourse should not be used as a means of bargaining to get your own way. Freely discuss your sexual relationships, especially sharing the things that you enjoy most, the things you can respond to and any hang ups you get. Discussing them openly is probably 90% of conquering them. God intends our sex life to be exciting and adventurous. We need our minds liberating from the concept that intercourse is limited to ten o'clock at night, in bed with the lights out!

Television can destroy successful sexual relationships. This is an area where we need real discipline. Many couples sit up so late at night watching T.V. that they get overtired, and sexual relationships do not work right when we are overtired.

Be wary of the many negative seeds sown by other people, including relatives and even parents, usually folk whose own marriages are not a real success. Comments like 'Oh, it soon wears off after the honeymoon' or 'There is nothing very much in it' are often made. I would say, as one who has been married for many years that it never wears off, it gets better as your relationship matures! One dear couple, who work with us regularly on the team, have recently celebrated their Ruby Wedding anniversary and are as much in love as on the day they got married. They declare that their relationship is still growing, maturing and getting better. God says, 'Let your fountain be blessed and rejoice in the wife of your youth. As a loving deer and graceful doe, let her breasts satisfy you at all times; and always be enraptured with her love.' (Proverbs 5:19)

Another bad seed that can be sown, the effect of which is not often realized, but can take root in the heart of a wife, comes from someone who is frigid. 'Oh, there is nothing in it for the wife; only the husband gets anything out of it.' This is so very wrong. There is just as much for the wife as for the husband in their sexual relationship together. God created us and He did not create us so that one would receive more pleasure than the other. Therefore, reject any of these negative seeds.

One of the most important things to do is to read a good Christian book (and I underline that it should be written by Christians) on the subject. One which I strongly recommend is *Intended for Pleasure,* by Ed and Gay Wheaton. This should be read by the couple a month before the actual date of the wedding. They should both read the book and then discuss it together, chapter by chapter as they go through it. After the wedding day, it is good to keep it in the home as a text book that you can refer to at any time.

5. The Family

I believe that it is good for a couple to wait, if possible, at least two years before starting a family. This means that they can have plenty of time to get to know and to enjoy each other and begin to build a good strong family home for a baby to be born into. It will take those two years to make the necessary adjustments in life, for, as soon as the baby arrives there will be new adjustments to make.

This then raises the whole matter of birth control, on which there are many different and varied views. There is certainly nothing unscriptual about it. Good spiritual perception tells us that while the Bible does not say that we should use birth control, it is a principle that helps married life to be successful. It prevents overloading a family with many children too quickly, and also releases the couple from the fear of an untimely child. It is good, if possible, to talk to a Christian doctor about the methods which are godly and suitable.

6. Finally

During the last counselling session, I briefly take the couple through all the points covered before, reminding them of the principles, answering any questions and then taking them through the actual wedding service and rehearsal in the church building.

I teach them on the importance of praying and reading God's Word together every day and establishing family devotions. I suggest that they make it a really good and lively time, sharing with them that one of the most beautiful memories of my honeymoon is when Heather and I got to our destination, before we went to bed, kneeling together and reading God's Word and praying together.

If you wish to receive *regular information* about *new books*,
please send your name and address to:—

London Bible Warehouse
PO Box 123
Basingstoke
Hants RG23 7NL

Name: ....
Address: ....
....
....
....

I am especially interested in:—

Music/Theology/"Popular"
Paperbacks
Delete which do not apply

P.S. If you have ideas for new Christian Books or other products, Please write to us too!